CW01512903

THE COMPLETE BIBLE STORY BOOK FOR KIDS

True Bible Stories For Children About
The Old and The New Testament Every
Christian Child Should Know

Karen Jones

Copyright 2019 © Karen Jones

All rights reserved.

No part of this guide may be reproduced in any form without permission in writing from the publisher except in the case of review.

Legal & Disclaimer

The following document is reproduced below with the goal of providing information that is as accurate and reliable as possible.

This declaration is deemed fair and valid by both the American Bar Association and the Committee of Publishers Association and is legally binding throughout the United States.

Furthermore, the transmission, duplication or reproduction of any of the following work, including specific information, will be considered an illegal act, irrespective of if it is done electronically or in print. This extends to creating a secondary or tertiary copy of the work or a recorded copy and is only allowed with express written consent from the Publisher. All additional right reserved.

The information in the following pages is broadly considered to be a truthful and accurate account of facts, and as such, any inattention, use or misuse of the information in question by the reader will render any resulting actions solely under their purview. There are no scenarios in which the publisher or the original author of this work can be in any fashion deemed liable for any hardship or damages that may befall them after undertaking information described herein.

Additionally, the information in the following pages is intended only for informational purposes and should thus be thought of as universal. As befitting its nature, it is presented without assurance regarding its prolonged validity or interim quality. Trademarks that are mentioned are done without written consent and can in no way be considered an endorsement from the trademark holder.

Table of Contents

Book 1:

Bible Story Book for Kids: The Old Testament

True Bible Stories For Children About God And The Old Testament Every Christian Child Should Know

Introduction

To the parents and guardians of our readers:

This book will present stories from the Old Testament in an approachable way. It is meant to engage children's interest in the Bible, as well as teach them. We will show that the bible does not have to be boring or stuffy, it can be exciting!

The stories will be presented accurately to the original Bible stories. However, violence, frightening, and racy elements will be toned down as much as possible. Names of people and countries may be confusing.

I encourage you to listen to this book before you give it to your child. You can decide what is appropriate for your child; what you'd like to read to them, what you'll read together and discuss, what they can read alone, and what is better for them to skip until they get a little older.

Some content may be frightening. God, as depicted in the Old Testament, is not a kindly old man sitting on a cloud. He is domineering and can be cruel and vengeful. Although this was toned down significantly, it would not be true to the Bible to change.

The overall message of the Old Testament is that God wants to be among His people. He blesses those that love and obey him. It is not until people turn away from God that He becomes vengeful. The first time this happened was when Adam and Eve hid from God, and this theme continues through the Old Testament.

Although this book is lifted from the New American Standard Bible (NASB), it will be appropriate for all Christians.

Thank you for choosing the Bible Story Book For

Kids: True Bible Stories For Children About God And The Old Testament Every Christian Child Should Know. I hope this helps your child on their discovery of God.

Chapter 1: Creation

(Genesis 1)

In the beginning, there was nothing. The universe was empty. God decided that He would create heaven and the earth, where His followers would live. God declared, "Let there be light!" As the light began to shine throughout the universe, this became the first day. When the light began to fade away, this became the first night.

On the second day, when the light was shining again, God separated the sky from the emptiness of the universe. He named the sky "heaven." This is where He would live, watching the earth He planned to create.

On the third day, God created the earth. Hills, valleys, mountains, and oceans developed out of the shapeless mass. He filled the earth with grass, fruit trees, flowers, and plants of all shapes and sizes. God added water to the earth, some large oceans, some tiny streams. God named the earth "land," and the waters "seas."

On the fourth day, God gave sources to the light. He created the sun to shine during the day. The moon came next. It would provide a little light at night. God also created the stars to shine during the night. The creation of the sun and moon made days and nights, seasons and years.

On the fifth day, God created animals of all shapes and sizes. He filled the seas with fish. He made huge whales and tiny seahorses. Then He created birds to fly through the skies. Finally, God created animals to roam the lands, from the smallest mouse to the largest lion. He told them to "be fruitful and multiply."

On the sixth day, God created man and named him Adam. God formed Adam to look like Him. God used the dust of the earth to form Adam's body. To wake Adam up, God breathed His own life into him. God then created a woman and named her Eve. God told Adam and Eve that the earth, seas, and animals were theirs to rule over. God blessed them and said,

---

"Be fruitful and multiply, fill the earth and subdue it, and have dominion over the fish of the sea and over the birds of the air and over every living thing that moves upon the earth."

Genesis 1:28

God looked down at all He had created and thought it was good. On the seventh day, after doing all this work, God finally rested.

Chapter 2: Adam and Eve

(Genesis 2-3)

As mist filled the land and seas, God breathed His life into the dust from the land. From this dust, Adam was made. Although God was giving Adam control over all of the earth, He wanted him to have a special place to live. God planted beautiful flowers and trees bearing delicious fruits. He called this land Eden. Four Rivers ran through this land. God took Adam to the Garden of Eden and told him that he got to live there. God told Adam to care for the land. Adam should plant and grow more food.

God brought the animals He had created to Adam to help with the land. God did not feel like this was enough. Adam needed an equal partner! God put Adam into a deep sleep and took out one of his ribs. God healed Adam immediately; he felt no pain. From this rib, God created a woman and named her Eve. God presented Eve to Adam. Eve was to be Adam's wife. Although they wore no clothes, neither Adam nor Eve was embarrassed.

Adam and Eve were allowed control over the Garden of Eden, they could eat whatever they wanted. God gave them just one rule. God told Adam and Eve they could not eat, or even touch the fruit from the Tree of Knowledge of Good and Evil.

A serpent lived in the Garden of Eden with Adam and Eve. The serpent spoke to Eve, telling her that she should eat the fruit from the Tree of Knowledge. The serpent claimed that eating the fruit would give Eve all the knowledge that God had. She would know everything, of good and evil. Eve gave in and ate the fruit. She shared it with Adam. The fruit they ate opened their eyes.

They were ashamed to see they were naked! Adam and Eve tried to use the leaves from a fig tree to make clothing for themselves.

When Adam and Eve next heard God walking through the Garden of Eden, they were afraid and hid. Seeing their embarrassment, God knew that Adam and Eve had disobeyed Him. They tried to explain, telling God that the serpent had tricked them into eating the fruit.

God punished Adam, Eve, and the serpent for their actions. The serpent's punishment was that it, and all of its descendants, would spend their lives crawling through the dirt. Descendants are someone's children, their children, their children's children and so on. Humans would be afraid of the serpent and would try to harm it.

Eve's punishment was that having babies would be painful, and her husband would rule over her. Adam's punishment was that he would have to grow all of his own food, instead of picking fruit from the Garden of Eden.

"Cursed are you among all animals.... upon your belly you shall go, and dust you shall eat, all the days of your life... He will strike your head, and you will strike his heel... I will greatly increase your pangs in childbirth... yet your desire shall be for your husband, and he shall rule over you... In toil, you shall eat... all the days of your life... and you shall eat the plants of the field"

Genesis 3:14-18

Finally, God created clothes for Adam and Eve to wear. They were forced to leave the Garden of Eden. God placed an angel with a fiery sword to guard the entrance to the Garden of Eden. Adam and Eve, and their future children could never return.

God was sad that he had to make Adam and Eve

leave the Garden of Eden. He loved them and had created a paradise on earth for them to live in. But God had no choice. They had disobeyed Him, and hidden from Him. From this day forward, God would no longer be as close to the humans He created.

Chapter 3: Cain and Abel

(Genesis 4)

After Adam and Eve left the Garden of Eden, they had two sons. Cain was born first, followed by Abel. When they grew up, Cain was given the job of growing food in the fields, while Abel took care of their animals.

Cain made an offering to God of the grain he had grown, while Abel offered God a young sheep. God liked Abel's offering of the sheep better than the grain. God could tell that Cain was jealous of Abel, and his preferred offering. God warned Cain against the jealousy and hatred he was developing towards his younger brother.

Cain could not contain his jealousy. One day, Cain brought Abel to the fields with him and hit Abel in the head. Cain hit Abel so hard, that Abel never got up. Cain covered him and left him in the fields. Soon, God asked Cain where his brother was. Cain made the mistake of lying to God instead of confessing. He asked, "Am I my brother's keeper?"

Because God knows everything that happens in the heavens and the earth, He knew what Cain had done. God cursed Cain. Cain would no longer be able to plant grains in the fields because the fields were poisoned with his brother's blood. God told that Cain he would have to wander the lands for the rest of his life. He would never find a home.

Cain told God that his punishment was too much. He could not stand it! Cain feared that he would be killed by other people because of what he had done to his brother. Because Cain was also showing regret at what he had done, God took mercy on him. Although Cain's punishment was not taken away, God gave him a mark. This mark would protect Cain. If someone tried to harm Cain, the person would be harmed seven times as badly. Although Cain would be made to wander for a long time, he would eventually be allowed to find a home.

Cain sadly left his home and his parents. After wandering through the lands, he finally made a new home in a land called Nod. In Nod, Cain found a wife. Cain and his wife had a child named Enoch. Cain built a city, also naming it Enoch.

Adam and Eve had lost two sons. Abel was lost to violence, and Cain was lost to his punishment. They were also banned from the Garden of Eden. God loved them despite their mistakes and felt bad for them. God decided to bless them with another son. They named him Seth. Seth grew up to have his own son, who he named Enosh.

From the descendants of Enoch and Enosh, mankind began to fill the world. Although some of these people were good, too many were bad.

Chapter 4: Noah's Ark

(Genesis 6-9)

Several generations after Enoch and Enosh, the world was filled with people who sinned. These sinners did not have God in their lives. They did not worship God. They did wicked things God and to each other. After much thought, God decided that the only way to get rid of the evil in the world was to wash it away with a huge flood.

There were still some good people in the world. Noah was the great-grandson of Enoch, and he was a very good person. Noah also had a very nice family. God decided that Noah and his family should be spared from the flood. God visited Noah to warn him about the flood He was planning. God told Noah to build a huge ark. God gave Noah directions how the ark should be built. God also told Noah he would need to stock the ark with food for his family.

Although many people thought Noah was crazy for building this ark, he trusted in God completely. Noah's family believed him, so they helped him to build the ark. God loved the animals He had created, and wanted to save them. The animals were innocent. God sent the animals of the land and air, a male and female of each kind, to the ark. The animals for the sea would be fine in the flood! Noah was told by God what kind of food and care the animals would need to eat aboard the ark.

When the ark was completed, the animals were on board, supplies were loaded, it began to rain. Noah and his family boarded the ark and sealed the doors. The rain lasted for forty days! After forty days of rain, the sun began to shine once again, but all Noah could see was water. Flood water covered the earth for one hundred and fifty days. Everything was washed away. There was no more evil. The world was pure once more.

Finally, the ark came to a stop, on the top of Mount Ararat. Noah could not see any other land. Noah released a raven to see if it could find any land. The raven flew around, but came back soon; there were nowhere else for it to land. Noah then released a dove, but it did not find land either. Noah waited for a week, then he sent the dove out again. This time, the dove returned with an olive leaf! Noah knew that land was near and that soon they could get off the ark.

Noah waited one more week and released the dove again. This time, it did not come back. Noah knew that the dove had found land, and was making a new home. It was time for everyone to get off the ark, but Noah was nervous. What would the earth be like after the flood? God encouraged Noah to leave the ark, with all of his family and the animals, and make a new home, expanding over the freshly washed lands.

"Be fruitful and multiply, and fill the earth."
Genesis 8:1

Noah built an altar to God and burned offerings. Noah wanted to thank God for saving him and his family. God was pleased by the offering and promised that he would never again flood the earth.

"I establish my covenant with you, that never again shall all flesh be cut off by the waters of a flood, and never again shall there be a flood to destroy the earth.

Genesis 9:11

Chapter 5: The Tower of Babel

(Genesis 11)

God had told Noah that his descendants should spread through the earth, but they did not. Instead, most lived in a city called Shinar. At this time, all humans spoke the same language.

The people of Shinar began to believe in multiple false gods, not just God. Their city grew, and they decided to build a huge tower. They wished for their false gods to be able to use the tower as a bridge from heaven to the earth.

The people of Shinar wanted to show off to their false gods and become famous throughout the lands. They thought this would keep them from having to scatter themselves throughout the lands. They could stay together, and make the city even bigger. The people had turned away from their true God. Their pride was more important to them than the Lord.

When the tower was built, God came to the city of Shinar. He was angry with the people. God worried that because they all spoke the same language, they could accomplish anything. They would continue to turn away from Him. God decided He would spread the people of Shinar all over the earth, and confuse their language.

The people were no longer able to communicate with each other. Each group of people now spoke a different language. God renamed the city, Babel. Since the people could no longer talk to each other, they were forced to stop building up the city. Thus, people spread out and developed the land, as God had wished.

Chapter 6: The Life of Abraham

(Genesis 12-22)

Abram and Lot

When he was first born, Abraham's parents named him Abram. God commanded Abram to leave his home in Haran and develop a great nation. This nation would be filled with the people of God. God promised Abram that if he obeyed, God would bless him, and his family for years to come. God would bless those who blessed Abram and curse those who cursed him.

Abram had great faith in God, so he obeyed. At the age of seventy-five, Abram took his wife, Sarai, and Lot, his nephew, and left Haran for the land of Canaan. When they reached Canaan,

God appeared. God gave the land of Canaan to Abram and his descendants. Abram built God an altar where He had appeared. He then moved onto the edge of the mountains in Bethel, and there he built another altar to God.

There was a famine in the land, so Abram and his family traveled to Egypt to find food. A famine is when people have a hard time growing food for a long time. It is a time when many people are very hungry.

Sarai was a very beautiful woman, so Abram asked her to say she was his sister. He was afraid the Egyptians would be too jealous if they knew she was his wife.

The Egyptians were amazed at Sarai's beauty. She was taken to the Pharaoh, who gave her gifts of camels, donkeys, sheep, oxen, and servants. God was angry with the Pharaoh for taking Sarai and cursed his home. When the Pharaoh figured out why God had cursed him, he was angry at

Abram for lying to him. The Pharaoh sent Sarai, and the gifts he had given her, back to Abram.

Abram, his family, and followed all left Egypt. They traveled to Negev and finally returned to Bethel. By now, Abram was very rich. Abram and Lot both had many tents, herds, and flocks of livestock. There was not enough room, and the fields could not produce enough food for both of them and all of their followers. This caused fights between the followers of Abram and Lot.

Abram and Lot still loved and respected each other very much. They decided to separate to stop the fighting between their followers. Lot took his followers to the valley of Jordan which was filled with plants and had plenty of water. Abram took his followers back to Canaan which God had already given to him. God then came to Abram again, giving him even more land. Abram took his followers and finally settled down in Mamre, where he built God another altar.

In nearby countries, several kings were at war. The people of Sodom and Gomorrah ran to the hills for safety. They took everything they could carry, including food. Lot, Abram's nephew, was living in Sodom at the time. He was captured and taken with them. The people of Sodom and Gomorrah had many captives.

One man was able to escape. He came to Abram and told him that his nephew was a captive. Abram gathered an army of three hundred and eighteen men and left for the hills to save Lot. Abram rescued Lot, and brought him home, along with the women and other captives.

Abram, Sarai, and Hagar

Abram was blessed with a beautiful wife, loving nephew, and many followers, but he was sad that he didn't have any children. God visited Abram in his tent and brought him outside. God asked Abram to count the stars, and told him that was how many descendants he would have! God asked Abram to bring him a three-year-old cow, goat, ram, a turtledove, and a young pigeon.

Abram brought God all the animals he asked for. In return, God told Abram that his descendants would be slaves in another land for four hundred years. But, they would be rewarded when they were free. The people who had enslaved them would be punished. God promised many lands to Abram and his descendants.

Abram and Sarai still had not been blessed with children. Sarai suggested that Abram have a baby with her maid, Hagar. When Hagar became pregnant, Sarai became very jealous and was mean to her. When Hagar could take this no longer, she ran away into the desert.

Luckily, Hagar soon came across a fresh spring. It was dangerous for a pregnant woman to wander the desert alone, especially when she had no water! While Hagar was resting by the spring, one of God's angels visited her! The angel asked

Hagar where she was going. When Hagar told the angel that she was hiding from Sarai because Sarai was cruel to her, the angel told Hagar to be brave and go home. She must be a good servant to Sarai. The angel told Hagar that when she gives birth, she should name her son Ishmael. The angel promised Sarai that God would watch over her and Ishmael if she obeyed these instructions.

Hagar returned home and soon gave birth to Ishmael. Abram was eighty-six years old when he became a father.

Abram Becomes Abraham!

When Ishmael turned thirteen, God visited Abram again. God reminded Abram that He had made many promises to him. Abram was promised many descendants, and a lot of land for them to rule over. Then, God told Abram he was now named Abraham because he would be the father of many kings and nations. Sarai's name was changed to Sarah because she would be the mother of many kings and nations. God promised to watch over their descendants as long as they worshipped Him as their one true God. Abraham's family would be blessed throughout the years.

Later, three men suddenly appeared in front of Abraham's tent. Abraham thought they might be messengers from God! Abraham treated them as honored guests. Abraham asked Sarah to make a cake. He told a servant to prepare a meat dish. Abraham gathered milk and butter. The meal was presented to the three men.

After they ate, one of the men asked where Sarah was. Abraham answered that she was in the tent. The man then told Abraham that Sarah would have a son! Sarah overheard this conversation but thought she and Abraham were too old to have a child. She laughed at the possibility. God was displeased that Sarah had laughed.

When the three men left, Abraham knew they had been sent from God. He trusted in what they had told him. He was glad he had treated them with kindness and respect.

The Cities of Sodom and Gomorrah

In the cities of Sodom Gomorrah, the people were very wicked. They had turned away from God. They worshipped other gods and behaved horribly. They were cities full of sinners. God wanted to punish the cities.

God didn't know if He should tell Abraham His plans for the cities. God sent two angels to check on the city of Sodom while He talked with Abraham. God loved and respected Abraham, so decided to tell him what He had planned for Sodom and Gomorrah.

As they stood outside Abraham's tent and gazed down toward the city, Abraham asked God if the good people in the city would be punished along with the bad. Abraham argued that the innocent people in the city should be saved. God promised that if his messengers found fifty good people, the whole city would be saved. Abraham and God debated. Abraham got God to promise that if just ten good people were found, the whole city would be spared!

When the angels got to Sodom, they met Abraham's nephew, Lot. He invited them to his home for a feast and said they could stay the night. After they had dinner, the people of Sodom grouped around the house. They yelled at Lot and his visitors, taunting them. They told Lot to send his visitors out to sin with them.

Lot went to his doorway and asked the people of Sodom to leave his visitors alone. He told them not to be so wicked. But the people would not give up! They grabbed Lot and tried to break into the house. The angels helped Lot get safely back inside. When the door was shut, the wicked people trying to break in were suddenly blinded! Without sight, they could not find their way into the house. Lot, his family, and the visiting angels were safe for the night.

When they were safely locked in, the angels asked Lot if he had any more family in the city of Sodom. They warned Lot that they were going to destroy the city and its wicked citizens the next day. Lot warned the two men that were engaged to his two daughters of the coming destruction. The two men thought Lot was joking. They did not listen to his warning.

In the morning, the angels told Lot to take his family and leave, before the city was destroyed. The angels took them to the edge of the city and said that they must run to the hills. They should not stop, or look back. Lot was very grateful to the angels, for they had been very kind. Because of the angels, their lives would be saved! Lot was afraid he could not make it all the way to the hills. The angels agreed that Lot could take his family to the nearby small city of Zoar instead.

Soon after Lot and his family left Sodom, God made it rain fire in the cities of Sodom and Gomorrah. Lot's wife could not control her curiosity. She turned around to see what was happening. When she looked at the city, she became a pillar of salt.

Miles away, Abraham walked from his tent to where he had spoken with God about the city of Sodom. From this distance, he was able to safely look at the cities. He saw that they had become full of fire. Ten good people were not found in the city of Sodom. The angels of God saved the good people; Lot and his children.

Lot was afraid to stay in the city of Zoar, so he took his two daughters, and they found shelter in a cave. When his older daughter had a son, she named him Moab. The younger daughter also had a son named Ben-ammi.

Abraham Betrays Abimelech

Although Abraham was now very old, he continued to travel God's land. He once again claimed that Sarah was his sister and not his wife. Abimelech, King of Gerar, took Sarah. God was angry and spoke to Abimelech in his dreams. God threatened Abimelech and told him Sarah was married. Abimelech had not touched Sarah. He told God that he had been lied to by Sarah and Abraham, who claimed to be brother and sister.

God accepted that Abimelech had not meant any harm. God told Abimelech that if he gave Sarah back to Abraham, who was His prophet, that Abimelech would not be punished. However, if Abimelech kept Sarah, knowing now it was wrong, Abimelech and his whole family would be punished.

The next morning, Abimelech gathered his servants and told them about his dream. He also asked Abraham why he had lied. Abimelech gave Sarah back to Abraham, along with gifts of coins, sheep, oxen, and servants. He invited them to live wherever they wanted in his lands.

God rewarded Abimelech for his good deeds by blessing his household. His wife and female servants all had children. God still loved Abraham but was angry he had lied.

Isaac and Ishmael

God had made many promises to Sarah and Abraham that they would have children. Despite their old age, they finally had a son. He was named Isaac. To celebrate their happiness, Abraham threw a big party.

Hagar and Sarah had never gotten along after Hagar returned from the desert many years ago. Hagar was making fun of the baby Isaac during his party. Sarah was of course very angry. She made Abraham tell Hagar and her son Ishmael to leave.

Abraham was very sad to lose his son Ishmael but did what Sarah wished. He gave Hagar and her son water and asked them to leave. Abraham trusted that God must have a plan for them.

After Hagar and Ishmael walked a long way, they stopped for a break. They rested and drank the water Abraham had given them. Hagar walked away from Ishmael and cried. She was afraid the heat would make her son sick, and they had just finished all their water. God sent an angel to visit Hagar. The angel comforted her. He ordered Hagar to pick up Ishmael, and take good care of him. The angel promised that God had plans for Ishmael's future!

Hagar wiped away her tear and saw a well. It was filled with cool water! As the angel told her to do, Hagar lifted her son and gave him the cold water to drink. Ishmael felt better right away and was able to continue on their journey.

Hagar and Ishmael settled down in the wilderness. Ishmael became a skilled archer when he grew up. God watched over him his whole life.

The Greatest of Faith

Throughout his life, Abraham and God had made many promises to each other. God decided to test Abraham's faith. God told Abraham that he must take his son Isaac, and give him to God as an offering. Out of everyone in the world, Abraham loved Isaac most deeply. However, as much as he loved Isaac, he loved and trusted God.

Abraham loaded up his donkey with supplies, and with Isaac, went to the place God had demanded. Isaac asked what they were doing, and Abraham told him they were going to sacrifice a lamb to God. Isaac pointed out they did not have a lamb, but Abraham said that God would provide it.

When they reached their destination, Abraham built an altar and put Isaac on it. Before Abraham could offer Isaac to God, God stopped him. Abraham had proven to God that God was the most important thing in his life. No harm had to come to Isaac. God made a ram appear, and Abraham offered the ram to God. Abraham was very thankful that his son had been spared.

Once again, Abraham was rewarded. God promised that Abraham's family would fill the earth throughout the years. God swore He would watch over them, and bless them.

Chapter 7: A Bride for Isaac

(Genesis 24)

Isaac's mother Sarah lived to be one hundred and twenty-seven. Abraham, Isaac's father, was very old and his greatest wish was that his son Isaac be blessed with a happy family. Abraham wanted to see his son happily married before he joined Sarah in heaven.

Abraham asked his most trusted servant, Eliezer, to find a wife for his son. Eliezer was to find a woman who wanted to marry Isaac and would move to the lands that God had given to Abraham and his family. If Eliezer found a woman that would marry Isaac, but would not move to be with him, Eliezer was free of his duty. Isaac must not move away.

Eliezer loaded ten camels with supplies and traveled to Mesopotamia in search of a bride for Isaac. When he reached the city walls, Eliezer took a break from his journey. He gave his camels water and prayed to God. Eliezer asked God to show him who the best bride for Isaac would be. Young women were coming out from the city walls to get water from the well. Eliezer told God he would ask the women to borrow a pitcher for a drink. The right woman for Isaac will offer Eliezer water, and also get water for his camels. This would show that she had a kind heart.

Soon, a beautiful and innocent young woman came to the well. Her name was Rebekah. She was the daughter of Nahor, Sarah's brother. Eliezer asked Rebekah if he could borrow her pitcher so he could get a drink of water. Instead of loaning him a pitcher, Rebekah got water for Eliezer! While he rested and drank, she got more water, which she gave to his camels. Eliezer knew this would be the perfect wife for Isaac and his prayers were answered!

Eliezer asked Rebekah her name, and she told him. Eliezer presented her with a gold ring and two gold bracelets. He asked if there was room for him to stay at the home of her father. Rebekah told Eliezer there was plenty of room, with food, and straw for his camels. Eliezer was grateful to God that He had brought such a kind woman to him. He was very excited that he had found the perfect woman for Isaac so quickly.

Rebekah went home to tell her family about the man she had met. Her brother, Laban, went out to the well to meet Eliezer. Laban welcomed Eliezer to their home and helped him settle in. Laban also helped take care of the camels, giving them straw, food, and water.

Before Eliezer would accept his meal, he told the family why he was there. Eliezer explained that he was the servant of Abraham, a rich man who had been blessed by God. Eliezer also explained that Abraham wanted his son to have a wife from the land God has blessed, not Canaan, where he was currently living.

Eliezer also told the family that he had prayed to God about finding the right wife for Isaac, and how Rebekah was the answer to his prayers. Rebekah's family gave permission to Eliezer that he could take Rebekah to Isaac. Rebekah agreed to leave her family and move to be with her future husband. The whole family believed it was God's will! Eliezer presented the family with gifts of silver, gold, and beautiful clothes. Rebekah was given the best gifts of all. Finally, they all feasted together.

The next morning, Eliezer told Rebekah that it was time to go. Her family was sad to say goodbye and asked them to stay longer. Eliezer said they had to be on their way, Abraham must know his final wish would be fulfilled.

It took many days for Eliezer and Rebekah to travel from Mesopotamia to Canaan. Rebekah was very nervous but excited to start her new life. She was looking forward to meeting her new family, especially her future husband. Rebekah wondered what Isaac would be like. She was confident that she was doing what God wanted.

When they were very close to home, Rebekah saw a man in the fields and asked Eliezer who it was. It was Isaac! Rebekah covered herself with her veil and got down from her camel. It was love at first sight for Isaac and Rebekah. Eliezer told Isaac the story of his trip. Abraham was very happy with Eliezer's choice when he met Rebekah. He loved her too. Rebekah and Isaac were soon happily married!

Chapter 8: Jacob & Esau

(Genesis 25-27)

After Rebekah and Isaac married, they continued to live in Abraham's home. It took a long time for them to have children, but they were finally blessed with twins! Esau was born first, followed quickly by Jacob. Jacob was holding Esau's heel as they were born.

Even though they were twins, the boys were very different. Esau was big, strong, hairy, and liked to be outdoors. He was a very good hunter and cooked the meat just how his father liked it. Isaac was very proud of Esau. He loved both his sons, but couldn't help favoring Esau, his firstborn.

Jacob was smaller, quieter, not hairy, and smarter. He spent more time in the tent, helping his mother. Rebekah loved both her sons, but couldn't help favoring Jacob. Esau was just so rough! Even though Esau was born first, Jacob thought he deserved the birthright. Jacob believed he would be a better head of the family, and his mother agreed.

One day, Esau returned home after an unsuccessful hunting trip. He was very tired and hungry. Jacob had been making lentil stew that day. Esau asked Jacob for some stew. Jacob cleverly took advantage of how tired and hungry Esau was. Jacob said that he would give Esau some stew if Esau gave Jacob his birthright. Esau was too hungry to think straight, so he accepted this deal.

Once he had eaten and was thinking more clearly, Esau was very angry that he had been tricked into selling his birthright for a bowl of stew. Esau came to hate his birthright and his twin brother.

Jacob had sneakily tricked Esau out of his birthright, but this was not enough. Now he wanted his father's blessing. This blessing was meant for the oldest son. By this time, Isaac was very old, and couldn't see well. Rebekah helped Jacob figure out a way to trick his father into giving Jacob the blessing meant for Esau.

One day, Isaac felt the end of his long life was near. He asked Esau to hunt for him, and prepare the meat just the way he liked it. He promised that he would eat the meal, then give Esau his blessing. Esau obeyed his father and headed out into woods for the perfect animal. He wanted to make this special for his father.

Rebekah overheard Isaac and Esau talking. She told Jacob to bring her meat from their livestock. She would make this into a meal while Esau was hunting. Rebekah then dressed Jacob in Esau's clothes so that he smelled like Esau. She put skins on his hands so that he felt as hairy like

Esau.

When Jacob took Isaac his meal, dressed in Esau's skins, Isaac was suspicious. It sounded like Jacob, but the hands felt like Esau. Jacob insisted that he was Esau. Finally, Isaac began to eat. After his meal, Isaac asked for a kiss. Jacob kissed his father's cheek. When Jacob was that close, Isaac could smell Esau's clothes. This convinced him that Jacob really was Esau. Isaac blessed Jacob, disguised as Esau. Isaac blessed him with success, fruitful harvests, and as a ruler. Isaac cursed anyone who would hurt Jacob.

"May God give you the dew of heaven,

And the fatness of the earth,

And an abundance of grain and new wine;

May peoples serve you,

And nations bow down to you;

Be master of your brothers,

And may your mother's sons bow down to you.

Cursed be those who curse you,

And blessed be those who bless you."

Genesis 27:28-29

Now having received his blessing, Jacob left his father. Soon, Esau got home with the meat from his hunt. He prepared Isaac's favorite meal. When Esau presented the meal to Isaac, he was confused. He thought that he had just eaten Esau's meal, and blessed him. But then, Isaac and Esau realized they had been tricked. Both Isaac and Esau were very upset. Isaac gave a blessing to Esau, but he could not take back the blessing that Jacob had stolen.

Esau was very angry with Jacob. He had been tricked out of his birthright and his father's blessing by his brother! Esau plotted revenge but decided he would wait until his father was gone. He loved his father very much and did not want to upset Isaac in his last days.

Rebekah overhead Esau's plans, and warned Jacob. She told Jacob that he should leave, and find her brother, Laban, who lived in Haran. Rebekah told Jacob he must stay there until Esau's anger had faded. She promised she would send for him when this happened.

Rebekah tried to hide her part in tricking Esau out of his blessing She told Isaac that she was sending Jacob away so that he could find a wife in other lands. She did not like the women she knew in Canaan. But really, she did not want to lose her son and husband at the same time.

Chapter 9: Jacob and His Family

(Genesis 28-33)

Jacob Leaves Home

I saac called his son Jacob to him. He gave him a final blessing, telling him that he should not marry one of the women in Canaan. Isaac told Jacob to travel to Haran, and find his Uncle Laban. One of Laban's daughters should become Jacob's wife. Isaac asked God to bless Jacob, that He would give him a big family, a lot of lands, and many followers.

Jacob left home and began his journey to Haran. He spent many nights camping, using only stones for pillows. He took the long way because he was very afraid that his twin brother would follow him, looking for revenge. Jacob missed his home, his father, and most of all, his mother. He was afraid he would never be able to go home again.

One night, Jacob lay down, resting his head on a stone. That night, he had a dream. In his dream, he saw a ladder so tall that it reached heaven. On the ladder, there were many angels. Some were climbing up to heaven, others were climbing down to earth. God stood above the ladder and spoke to Jacob. God declared, "I am God. The God of Abraham and the God of your father, Isaac." God told Isaac that He was giving him the land he was sleeping on. The land would belong to him and all his descendants. Jacob's descendants would spread through the land, and be blessed.

When Jacob woke up, he was both afraid and grateful. He thought he was at the gate to heaven! Jacob built an altar to God and named the land Bethel. When the altar was completed,

Jacob resumed his travels.

One day, Jacob came across three shepherds and their flocks of sheep by a well. Jacob asked where they were from, and they answered, "Haran." This is where Jacob was headed! He asked if he knew Laban. They did know Laban and pointed out a beautiful woman headed their way. It was Rachel, the daughter of Laban, who was coming with her sheep to get water from the well.

Jacob helped Rachel get water for her sheep, and then he kissed her! Finally, he introduced himself as Jacob, son of Rebekah, the sister of her father. They went to find Laban, who welcomed Jacob into his home.

Jacob stayed with Laban and his family for a month. Rachel had an older sister, named Leah. It was traditional for the oldest daughter to be married first, but Jacob loved Rachel. Jacob promised Laban that he would work for him for seven years if Laban allowed him to marry

Rachel. He loved her so much, seven years went by quickly. He was very excited to marry her!

Jacob Gets Married

After seven years, Jacob told Laban he had done his time, and now wanted to marry Rachel. Laban threw a feast to celebrate the marriage. However, that night, Laban tricked Jacob into marrying Leah instead of Rachel. Laban gave Leah a maid, Zilpah, as a wedding gift.

Jacob was very angry that he was tricked out of marrying his true love. Laban defended himself, saying the oldest daughter had to be married first. Laban said that Jacob had to work for one more week, then he could marry Rachel. Jacob would then have to stay and work for seven more years.

Jacob agreed and was finally able to marry his true love, Rachel. God felt sorry for Leah, because she was married but not loved. God gave

Leah a son, and she named him Reuben. She hoped this would make Jacob love her! She had three more sons, named Simeon, Levi, and Judah. Although Leah gave Jacob sons, his love for Rachel did not fade.

Rachel was very jealous that she did not have any children, while her sister had three. Rachel decided that she would have her maid, Bilhah, carry her baby for her. Bilhah had two sons for Rachel, named Dan and Naphtali.

Leah could have no more children, so she too had her maid carry her babies. Zilpah had two sons for Leah, named Gad and Asher.

Then a miracle happened! Leah could have babies again. She had two more sons, named Issachar and Zebulun. She also had a daughter named Dinah.

God felt it was only fair to let Rachel have more babies too. She had one more son and named him Joseph.

By now, the seven years Jacob promised to Laban had gone by. Jacob asked for Laban's blessing for him to take his wives and children and leave. Laban did not want them to go even though Jacob had served him for many years. Jacob was determined to leave. He was tired of working for the father of his wives. Laban did not give him fair pay.

Jacob never forgot that Laban tricked him into marrying Leah. During Jacob's time working for Laban, the flocks of sheep, cows, and camels had grown. Jacob took his fair share of the flock and left the rest with Laban.

Jacob Returns Home

God told Jacob to take his family, servants, and flocks back to his home in Canaan. This land belonged to his brother Esau, and Jacob was still very afraid of him. When he got close to Canaan,

Jacob sent messengers to his twin brother, to let him know he was coming.

When the messengers returned, they reported that Esau was coming to meet Jacob. Esau was bringing four hundred men with him. Jacob was very scared. He thought Esau was bringing those men to attack him. Jacob prayed to God for safety and prepared gifts for Esau. Jacob selected a hundred of goats, sheep, and donkeys to give his brother.

When Esau arrived, he ran to meet Jacob. Jacob was terrified, but Esau hugged him and kissed his cheeks. Over the years, Esau had forgiven Jacob. Both brothers cried. Esau kindly refused the gift of animals Jacob offered him. Esau appreciated that Jacob wanted to give him gifts, but he did not need them. Esau had been blessed by God and had plenty himself.

After they had talked, the brothers decided to go their separate ways. Jacob took his family, animals, and servants, and traveled to Succoth. Esau took his family, animals, and servants, and made his home in Seir. This time, the brothers parted as friends.

Chapter 10: Joseph Is Betrayed

(Genesis 37)

Soon after returning to his homeland, Jacob lost his beloved Rachel, and his father, Isaac. Although Jacob was very sad, he was comforted by his daughter and twelve sons. He loved them all, but some were hard to be proud of. Jacob was most proud of his son, Joseph. Joseph was one of his youngest sons, and the last child his beloved Rachel had given him.

Because Jacob missed Rachel so much, he sometimes spoiled her youngest son, Joseph, more than his other children. Naturally, this caused jealousy among the siblings. Joseph was also very different from most of his brothers. They did not understand him. What they did not understand, they disliked. While his brothers were happiest outside, tending the fields, Joseph spent most of his time inside, helping his mother, and thinking.

One day, Jacob gave Joseph the gift of a beautiful coat which is made of many colors. His brothers did not have a beautiful garment like this. His brothers were very jealous. Their dislike and jealousy of Joseph began to turn to hate.

Joseph had many dreams and ideas and made the mistake of telling them to his brothers. One night, Joseph had a dream that he was working with his brothers in the fields, and his bundle of grain rose straight into the air. The bundles of grain his brothers were working on gathered around Joseph's bundle and bowed to it. Joseph told his brother about this dream. His brothers thought the dream meant Joseph planned to rule them. They resented Joseph even more.

Joseph had another dream that eleven stars, the

sun, and the moon bowed down to him. When he told his father, he was scolded. He should be more humble. When he told his brothers, they began to plot against him.

Not long after this dream, Joseph's brothers were working in the fields. Jacob, Joseph's father, sent Joseph to the fields with a message for his brothers. The brothers saw their chance! They decided that when Joseph got to them, they would throw him in a pit, and wild animals would eat him. Reuben, Joseph's oldest brother, tried to talk the other brothers out of letting animals eat Joseph. Reuben hoped that when the other brothers left, he could pull Joseph out of the pit.

When Joseph reached his brothers, they took his beautiful coat, and threw him into the pit, without food or water. Then they sat down to have some lunch. As they were eating, a group of men stopped to talk to them. These men were on their way to Egypt.

Judah, one of the brothers, suggested that they sell Joseph to this group. They were strangers, and would probably never see them again! They could safely get rid of Joseph, without having to hurt them. The other brothers agreed, so they sold Joseph into slavery.

The brothers didn't know what they would tell their father about Joseph's disappearance. Finally, they tore up the multicolored coat and smeared it with animal blood. They told their father Joseph was attacked by a wild animal, and this coat was all that remained.

Jacob was very sad. He mourned for his youngest son. His other children tried to comfort him, but his sorrow was too great.

Chapter 11: Joseph's Egyptian Adventure

(Genesis 39-42)

Joseph Is Jailed

When Joseph got to Egypt, he was sold to Potiphar. Potiphar was good and a fair man, and the captain of the Pharaoh's bodyguards. Potiphar liked and trusted Joseph. Potiphar soon made Joseph the head of the servants in his household.

Joseph was young and handsome. He was very likable. Unfortunately, Potiphar's wife liked Joseph too much. She tried to make him forget that she was a married woman. Joseph refused to betray Potiphar or God. This hurt Potiphar's wife's feelings. Her hurt feelings quickly turned to anger.

Joseph continued to resist Potiphar's wife. She would not give up. One day, she grabbed his robes as he tried to get away from her. He left the robes and ran. Potiphar's wife screamed and used to robes to trick Potiphar. She convinced Potiphar that Joseph had betrayed him, and she had resisted. She claimed she had escaped by taking his robes and running.

Potiphar was furious with Joseph and threw him in jail. God knew Joseph had been betrayed by first by his brothers and then by Potiphar's wife. God blessed Joseph while he was in jail. This caused the chief jailer to be kind to Joseph, and trust him. Joseph was put in charge of some of the other prisoners, who also liked him.

Two of the men Joseph became friends with in the jail had high positions in the Pharaoh's household. They had not committed a crime but had merely annoyed the Pharaoh. One was the chief butler, and the other the chief baker.

One night, the chief butler had a dream that he

saw a grapevine with three branches. As he watched, the grapes began to grow! When they were ripe, he crushed them into juice, which he gave to the Pharaoh. He told Joseph about this dream. Joseph told the chief butler that his dream meant that in three days, the Pharaoh would release him from jail, and invite him back to the palace.

The chief baker was very interested in what Joseph had told the chief butler. The chief baker told Joseph about a dream he had the night before. The chief baker had dreamed that he was carrying three loaves of bread to the Pharaoh. Birds had swooped down and eaten the bread before the chief baker reached the Pharaoh. Joseph was sad to tell the chief baker on what he thought this dream meant. Finally, Joseph admitted what he thought it meant. In three days, the Pharaoh would remove the chief baker's head.

Three days later, it was the Pharaoh's birthday. He threw a large feast for his servants. Both of

Joseph's predictions came true. Quickly becoming busy serving the Pharaoh, the chief butler forgot about his new friend Joseph, and the predictions he had made.

Joseph Is Freed!

Two years after the Pharaoh pardoned the chief butler, he had an odd dream. In the first dream, the Pharaoh saw seven fat healthy cows grazing by the Nile. Seven skinny unhealthy cows snuck up behind the healthy cows and ate them! The Pharaoh awoke, very upset. When the Pharaoh fell back asleep, he had another dream. There were seven plump and juicy ears of grain on a stalk. A wind brought in another seven ears. These ears were skinny and dry. The skinny ears swallowed the plump ears.

The Pharaoh searched far and wide for someone to tell him what the dreams meant. He summoned wise men from all corners of his lands. No one could tell him what the dreams meant. Finally, the chief butler remembered Joseph! The chief butler told the Pharaoh about the kind young man he met in jail, who correctly interpreted dreams.

The Pharaoh immediately called for Joseph. The Pharaoh asked Joseph what his dream meant. Joseph told the Pharaoh that God tells him what dreams mean, that it was not his own talent. The Pharaoh described his dreams for Joseph. God told Joseph what the dreams meant, and Joseph told the Pharaoh. Both dreams had the same meaning. For seven years, Egypt's land would be very fertile, and the people would be able to grow more food than they could eat. This would be followed by seven years of not being able to grow any food. Egypt and the surrounding lands would suffer a famine. Through Joseph, God advised the Pharaoh to pick someone to oversee the lands and save food for the famine.

Joseph Rules!

The Pharaoh trusted in what he had learned from Joseph and God. He felt Joseph was so wise that he picked him to oversee the lands. The Pharaoh took off his own ring and put it on Joseph's finger. He also gave Joseph beautiful clothes and other jewelry. Although the Pharaoh kept his title, Joseph was made a ruler too. All Egyptians had to obey him. Only the Pharaoh had more authority.

The Pharaoh renamed Joseph, Zaphenath-paneah. Asenath, a daughter of a high priest, was found to be Joseph's wife. Joseph was now thirty, and had quickly risen from prisoner in Egypt to ruler of Egypt!

For the next seven years, Joseph traveled throughout Egypt. He collected so much food that it could not be measured. It would be like trying to count the sand in the desert! He gathered one-fifth of what all the people of Egypt grew, except for the priests. The priests were allowed to keep everything they grew.

After seven years of fruitful growth in the fields, famine struck quickly. The Pharaoh sent all the Egyptians to Joseph, from whom they bought food. The famine wasn't just in Egypt. People from many lands began to come to Egypt to buy food.

Joseph Sees His Brothers

In Canaan, where Joseph's father and siblings lived, food had run out. Jacob heard rumors that there was food in Egypt. He sent all ten of his sons, except for the youngest, Benjamin. Now that Joseph was gone, Benjamin had become his father's favorite.

When the brothers reached Egypt, they did not realize that the rich man with the fancy clothes who controlled the food was their brother, Joseph. But Joseph did recognize them! Joseph wanted to know if they had changed in the past few years. He tried to figure out if they were still the type of men who would sell their brother into slavery. Joseph pretended to think that they were spies. Joseph instructed them to return with their younger brother while one of the brothers stayed in prison in Egypt.

The brothers discussed what to do in their own language. They did not know that Joseph could understand, for it was his language as well! The brothers said they were being punished for their sins against Joseph. When Joseph heard that, he knew they had changed. Simeon, one of the brothers, was put in prison, as the other brothers left to get Benjamin.

When the brothers were given sacks of grain, Joseph put their money back into the sacks. When the brothers got home and opened the sacks, they were afraid when they saw the money. How did it get there? Would they be accused of stealing?

Jacob refused to let the brothers take Benjamin to Egypt. He was afraid something bad would happen to his youngest son. He had already lost his beloved wife Rachel, and favorite son, Joseph! Poor Simeon remained an Egyptian prisoner.

Chapter 12: Joseph's Forgiveness

(Genesis 43-48)

W hen the grain had all been eaten, there was no other choice. The brothers, including Benjamin, all traveled back to Egypt. Jacob sent everything he could as presents to give the ruler in Egypt. Jacob hoped this would keep him from harming or keeping Benjamin and Simeon.

When the brothers got back to Egypt, Joseph saw they had brought Benjamin with them. Joseph was pleased they had obeyed him. Joseph instructed his servants to prepare a meal for him and the group of brothers. When the brothers spoke to Joseph, they presented him with gifts, money for grain, and the money they had found in the sacks. They admitted that their money had been returned to them, but they did not know how. They apologized and were clearly afraid. Joseph told them not to worry, it was a gift from God.

Simeon was released from prison and joyfully reunited with his brothers. Joseph asked the brothers how their father was. They answered that he was doing well. Finally, Joseph spoke to Benjamin and asked if this was the youngest brother. When told yes, Joseph blessed Benjamin. The brothers then all feasted together, though Joseph had still not revealed his true identity.

The next morning, the brothers were preparing to go back home to Canaan. Joseph told his servants to put all the money that they had paid back into their sacks. He also told them to put Joseph's silver cup in the sack of the youngest, Benjamin. He was still not quite ready to tell them his true identity.

When the brothers were barely beyond the city walls, Joseph sent his servants to overtake them and "find" the stolen goods. They were instructed to ask why the brothers had repaid Joseph's kindness with stealing from him.

The brothers were brought back to Joseph's house. They bowed to Joseph in fear. Joseph said that they were all free to go, except Benjamin, in whose sack the cup was found. Benjamin would stay in Egypt as a slave. Judah began to plead with Joseph. Judah told Joseph how their father lost his beloved wife Rachel. She had left him a son named Joseph, who was already dead. Judah still did not realize he was telling Joseph about Joseph! He went on to say that Jacob could not bear to lose Benjamin, his youngest son.

Judah cried out that if they came back to Canaan without Benjamin, their father would die of heartbreak. He begged Joseph to let him stay and be a slave in Benjamin's place. At this,

Joseph knew his brothers had truly changed. They were no longer bad men who would sell their younger brother into slavery. Instead, they would protect their brother.

Joseph asked his brothers to gather closer to him. At last, he announced, "I am Joseph!" The brothers were all afraid. But Joseph kissed them all. Joseph told his brothers he forgave them all, and that it was God's way of bringing him to Egypt.

Joseph then told his brothers about the exciting years he had spent in Egypt. From his time as a trusted servant to his downfall as a prisoner for two years to his sudden promotion to a ruler!

Joseph asked his brothers to return home to Canaan. He wanted them to tell their father that he was alive, well, and ruling Egypt! He said he hoped his brothers would bring Jacob back to Egypt with them. He promised them the best lands he could give them. They were given money, food, donkeys, and clothing for their father on his journey.

Jacob could hardly believe his ears when his sons returned with news of Joseph. When he saw the supplies Joseph had sent for the journey, he was convinced. He agreed to travel to Egypt. Jacob wanted nothing more than to be reunited with his son Joseph before he died.

Jacob and his daughters, sons, and their families packed quickly. Soon, they were ready to return to Egypt for the third time. When Joseph heard that his father and brothers were on their way, he drove his chariot past city gates to meet them.

Joseph ran to his father and hugged him tightly. Jacob cried that he was ready to die, now that he had finally seen Joseph again. But it was not to be. Jacob would live for many happy years in Egypt with his whole family!

When Joseph introduced his father brothers to

the Pharaoh, they asked if they could live in Egypt. Their family wanted to be close together after their long separation. The Pharaoh agreed and invited them to settle in the best land that Egypt had.

The famine continued. People ran out of money to buy grain from Joseph. They had to sell their livestock and land. Joseph greatly expanded the Pharaoh's lands during this time. Joseph was not greedy. He gave seeds to the people to plant. In return, the people were to give one-fifth of the harvest to the Pharaoh. This would leave the Egyptian people with plenty of food for their households.

When Jacob had reached the age of one hundred and forty-seven, he knew the end of his time on earth was near. He called for his son Joseph. His last wish was not to be buried in Egypt but in the home of his ancestors.

Before Jacob's last day, he requested that Joseph

come to see him. Jacob asked to see his grandsons, the boys Joseph had fathered in Egypt. He blessed them both, with many descendants, and many lands.

Chapter 13: Moses' Birth

(Exodus 1-2)

The Pharaoh the Joseph served was a good man. Although he could get angry at times, overall he was a fair and kind ruler. After he died, other kings followed. After a long time, there was a Pharaoh who no longer remember Joseph, a Hebrew, who was a wonderful ruler and did many good things for the land of Egypt. The number of Joseph's descendants had increased greatly over the years, and the Pharaoh feared they might take over.

Joseph's descendants, the Hebrews, began to be treated badly in Egypt. They were given all the hardest jobs and were not paid well. Over the years, they became slaves to the Egyptian people.

A particularly horrible Pharaoh rose to power.

This evil man instructed Hebrew midwives that Hebrew baby girls could be saved, but Hebrew baby boys must be thrown into the Nile!

Soon after this order, a Hebrew boy was born. The baby's mother hid him for as long as she could. After three months, she could hide him no longer. She went to the banks of the Nile and gathered reeds. She weaved a basket with the reeds she had collected. When the basket was complete, she covered it with tar so that no water could get in.

When the preparations were complete, the mother put her baby boy in the basket and put the basket in the Nile. She was heartbroken to lose her son, but this was the only way she could save his life.

The mother was too upset to watch what happened to her baby, but her daughter Miriam stayed. As Miriam lay hidden, she saw the Pharaoh's daughter and her maidens walk to the

Nile to bathe. The Pharaoh's daughter found the baby boy! She saw that he was a Hebrew child, but loved him immediately. No harm would come to this baby. She would raise him herself.

The baby had to be nursed, so the Pharaoh's daughter sent a maid to find a Hebrew woman who had recently given birth. The maid found the baby's mother. The Pharaoh's daughter asked her to nurse the baby boy for her, in return for payment.

The woman took her baby and took care of him until he was too old to nurse. At this time, he was returned to the Pharaoh's daughter, his adoptive mother. She decided to name him Moses.

Moses was raised as a prince. He had the best of everything life had to offer. When he was old enough, he learned that the Pharaoh's daughter was not his real mother. He had been adopted and was Hebrew by birth.

Although Moses loved his adoptive family, this made him think. He saw how the Hebrews were treated in Egypt. He did not understand why he lived in a palace, with his every need and want taken care of, while his true people were treated like slaves.

Moses decided to visit his true people in Egypt. He saw an Egyptian whip a Hebrew man who was working too slowly. Moses filled with such anger that he hit the Egyptian. Moses hit the man so hard that he did not get back up. Moses was scared of what he had done and covered him with sand.

The Pharaoh soon heard about Moses' crime. Before he was punished, Moses left the palace for good. He ran away to the mountains. Although he would miss living in luxury, he was now dedicated to helping his people.

Moses settled in Midian. He had managed to escape the Pharaoh and the men that were sent to catch him. One day, he was sitting by a well and met seven beautiful women. They were sisters. Their father was Reuel, a priest in Midian. The sisters were taking care of Reuel's sheep. Shepherds soon arrived with their sheep and roughly pushed the girls aside. Moses defended the sisters and forced the shepherds to leave. Then Moses helped the sisters give water to all their sheep.

When the girls got home early that day, their father asked why. The girls told their father about the man from Egypt who had defended and helped them. Reuel sent the girls to invite Moses to dine with them. Moses accepted the invitation. Reuel was so grateful to Moses that he invited Moses to stay with them. Moses thankfully accepted this invitation.

During his stay with Reuel and his daughters, Moses fell in love! Reuel blessed the marriage of his daughter Zipporah to Moses. It was not long before they were blessed with a son whom they named Gershom.

Chapter 14: The Burning Bush

(Exodus 3)

While Moses was living happily in Midian with his wife and son, a Pharaoh even more wicked than the one Moses had known was ruling Egypt. When Moses learned that his people were being treated even more poorly than before, he knew he had to do something. Moses knew it was dangerous, but it was the right thing to do.

Moses didn't act immediately. He knew that he needed a good plan before going back to Egypt and challenging the Pharaoh. One day, while Moses was taking care of Reuel's sheep on the mountains, he saw a bush on fire. Although there were flames, the bush was not burning up.

As Moses investigated the mysterious fire, he heard a voice calling his name. The voice seemed to be coming from the bush! Moses answered, and the voice said,

---

"Do not come near here; remove your sandals from your feet, for the place on which you are standing is holy ground...
I am the God of your father, the God of Abraham, the God of Isaac."
Exodus 3:5-6

Moses was so shocked that God was speaking to him that he hid his face! God viewed this as a sign of respect, so He continued. God told Moses that He had seen the suffering of Hebrews in Egypt. God wanted to save them from oppression by the Egyptians. Moses would help Him do this. God continued, assigning Moses the task of freeing the Hebrews from the Egyptians. God planned to send Moses to the new, evil Pharaoh and demand the release of the Hebrew people. Moses resisted, saying that he could not do it; he was too afraid! Although God was disappointed in Moses' reaction, He still loved him and believed in him. God promised that He would send Aaron, the brother of Moses, to help. Despite Moses' self-doubt, God still believed he could free the Hebrews by himself.

Chapter 15: The Ten Plagues of Egypt

(Exodus 6-12)

It was not a surprise to anyone that the Pharaoh denied Moses' request to free the Hebrews. If anything, the request angered him and made him crueler. But neither Moses nor God would give up. God had a plan. He had flooded the world, burned two cities. He was ready to try something new.

God told Moses to speak with the Pharaoh again. Moses was desperate. He did not think he was skilled at speaking. Why would the Pharaoh listen to him, when he had such a hard time getting the words out? God compromised with Moses again. God would speak to Moses, Moses would tell Aaron what God had said, and finally, Aaron would speak to the Pharaoh.

The first part of the plan was to demonstrate to the Pharaoh that Moses and Aaron truly were speaking for God. They hoped this would make the Pharaoh listen to what he was told.

When Aaron was speaking to the Pharaoh, he threw down his staff, and God turned it into a serpent. The Pharaoh summoned his wise men, and they threw down their staffs as well. These became serpents too, but not through the power of God! Aaron's staff which turned into a serpent ate all the other staffs which also turned into serpents. The Pharaoh was too Godless. He still did not believe Moses and Aaron were carrying a message from God.

Plague 1: River of Blood

After consulting with God, Moses and Aaron were ready for the next step. They were to unleash the first plague of Egypt! When the Pharaoh came down to the Nile the next morning, Moses and Aaron were waiting. Moses said, "Let my people go!" Aaron lifted his staff over the Nile, and God turned the water into blood.

As a result of the first plague, all the fish in the water died. No one could drink from the river, or water their fields. The Egyptians had to quickly dig wells. The Pharaoh remained unimpressed. His sorcerers could also change water. Seven days passed, and the Nile slowly cleared.

Plague 2: Frogs Fill the Land

Next, God told Moses and Aaron to tell the Pharaoh that unless the Pharaoh free the Hebrews, frogs would fill the land. Swarms will fill every home, the Nile, and the palace. Moses cried, "Let my people go!" The Pharaoh again refused, so Aaron lifted his staff above the Nile. Millions of frogs came hopping out of the Nile and started spreading throughout the land. Since the magicians of Egypt could do the same thing, the Pharaoh was not impressed.

The Pharaoh quickly grew tired of having his lands filled with frogs. He called for Moses and Aaron and agreed to let the Hebrews go if they got rid of the frogs. Moses told God what the Pharaoh had said, so God began taking away the frogs. By the next morning, most of the frogs had gone. The Pharaoh decided the frogs just left and betrayed his promise. He kept Moses' people as slaves.

Plague 3 and 4: Insects Infest the Land

God was very angry that the Pharaoh had ignored his promise. God instructed Moses to tell Aaron to hit the ground with his staff. When Aaron did this, gnats flew out of the dust, landing on every man, woman, child, and animal. The Pharaoh commanded that the magicians make gnats appear. The magicians could not. They claimed that it was a power God had, but they did not. The Pharaoh refused to listen.

The next morning, Moses and Aaron were waiting for the Pharaoh by the Nile. They said, "Let my people go! If you do not, your lands will fill with flies." When the Pharaoh did not free the Hebrews, Egypt began to fill with flies. Soon, every person, animal, and plant were covered with flies.

The Pharaoh was soon overwhelmed with misery. It was horrible being constantly swarmed with flies, and being served food that was also covered with the horrible insects! The Pharaoh called for Moses and Aaron. This time, he said that the Hebrews could go on a short journey to worship God. They could not go far, just to where Moses had seen the burning bush. However, as soon as God brought in a wind to blow away the flies, the Pharaoh changed his mind, and the Hebrews weren't allowed to leave.

Plague 5 and 6: Cursed Cattle and Bodies of Boils

Since the first three plagues were not successful, God decided it was time for harsher plagues. God instructed Moses and Aaron to tell the Pharaoh that if he did not free the Hebrews, all the livestock belonging to the Egyptians would die. Again, the Pharaoh refused. By the next day, all livestock belonging to the Egyptians had died. None of the livestock belonging to the Hebrews had been harmed. The Pharaoh was still not swayed. He would not let Moses' people go.

God instructed Moses to throw handfuls of soot into the air. He was to do this in front of the Pharaoh. As the ash slowly spread and fell to the ground, it caused boils and sores to develop on every Egyptian and all of their animals that had survived the previous plague.

The Pharaoh asked his magicians the replicate

what he thought was a spell. The magicians could not do it. They were also covered with painful boils, and could not perform any spells. The Pharaoh, though also covered with horrible boils, refused to free the Hebrews. He refused to believe that God was sending the plagues.

Plague 7: Hail, Fire, and Thunder

This time, God sent thunder, hail, and fire. The land of Egypt suffered from a terrible storm, except for Goshen, where the Hebrews lived. Even the Pharaoh was terrified. He called for Moses and Aaron. The Pharaoh admitted that he had been wicked. He said that if God stopped the storm, he would free God's people. Moses and Aaron were filled with hope. They asked God to stop the storm. As the storm faded, the Pharaoh forgot his terror. He refused to let the Hebrews go!

Plague 8: Swarms of Locusts

God sent Moses and Aaron back to the Pharaoh. They demanded to know how long the Pharaoh would refuse to believe in the power of God. When would the Hebrews be freed? The Pharaoh show no signs of being humbled, nor did he show any desire to free the Hebrews. God had Moses lift his staff over the land. All day and night, there was a swift wind coming from the east. In the morning, the wind was filled with locusts.

The locusts covered everything in sight. They ate all the plants, fruits, and trees. There was no color in sight, just the black of their buzzing bodies. The only place in the land that still had any green was in Goshen, where the Hebrews lived.

The Pharaoh, hungry and scared, called for Moses and Aaron. He apologized for his sins and asked them to take away the locusts. If they did, the Pharaoh would let their people go. God brought a west wind through Egypt, blowing the locusts into the Red Sea. Once the locusts were gone, the Pharaoh changed his mind again. The Hebrews must stay in Egypt.

Plague 9: Darkness Descends

God instructed Moses to reach his staff toward the sky. This would cause darkness to fall over all of Egypt. Moses obeyed, and for three days, Egypt was filled with complete darkness. However, the Hebrews had light in their homes. Once again, the Pharaoh called for Moses. The Pharaoh tried to make a deal. He said the Hebrews, man, women, and children, could leave. But, they must leave all of their livestock. Moses said that they needed their livestock as an offering for God. The Pharaoh would not accept this and sent Moses away.

The Pharaoh yelled that he never wanted to see Moses again. Moses agreed; the Pharaoh would never see him again. The Pharaoh furiously told

Moses that if he was seen again, he would be killed.

Plague 10: The Final Plague

God finally had to unleash a final, terrible plague. God did not want to do this, but he had to save his people from slavery. God planned to kill every firstborn; people and animal. In order to save themselves from this tragic plague, Moses told all the Hebrew families to sacrifice one of their livestock. To show that they were one of God's people, they were to use the blood to paint the doorposts. This would cause the plague to pass by their homes.

At midnight, the plague struck. Many people died, including the Pharaoh's son. Cries of sorrow could be heard through the land. Unknown to the Egyptians, the Hebrews were ready. They had eaten a large dinner, were dressed, packed, and ready to leave. In the darkness, Moses finally led his people out of

Egypt. As they left, they took gold, silver, and clothing from the Egyptians. They did not view this as stealing. They considered this rightful payment they had earned, for all their hard work over the years.

Chapter 16: Escaping Egypt

(Exodus 13-18)

The Red Sea Splits in Two!

Despite his sorrow, the Pharaoh was furious when he discovered the Hebrews had left Egypt. He immediately gathered an army of six hundred men and had his own chariot prepared. The Pharaoh led his army as they began to chase Moses and his people.

Moses had led his people all through the night. They walked as fast as they could. When they reached the banks of the Red Sea, they stopped to take a break. During this break, they looked back toward Egypt. They could see huge clouds of dust and knew they were being chased. They were afraid and began to complain. They had been led away from Egypt, only to be captured and punished!

Moses asked his people to remain calm. God would save them! God spoke to Moses, telling him to lead his people on. God told Moses to raise his staff over the Red Sea. When Moses obeyed, a strong wind blew, and the sea split in two! Moses led his people through the sea. The Pharaoh and his army followed. They were getting closer all the time.

When Moses and his people reached the other side of the sea, they were still ahead of the Egyptians. God advised Moses to raise his staff over the sea once again. When Moses did this, the winds calmed, and the sea returned to normal. The Pharaoh, his army, and all over their chariots were washed away.

When the Hebrews saw what Moses had done, they were overjoyed. They had been saved! They now fully accepted Moses as their leader. They were sure that God had been working through him. Although their belief had strengthened, they also feared the power of God. They had witnessed how strong his power was.

Moses and his people sang a song of thanks to God. Miriam, Aaron's sister, led the women in a dance.

"The Lord is my strength and song,
And He has become my salvation.
This is my God, and I will praise Him.
My father's God, and I will extol him...
Pharaoh's chariots and army He has cast into the sea...
In Your lovingkindness, You have led the people whom You have redeemed...
The Lord shall reign forever and ever."
Exodus 15:2-18

A Forty Year Journey

Although the Hebrews were freed, they were not yet home. They still had a long, hard journey ahead of them. But now, they had faith in God, and Moses to lead them. This kept them going even though they were traveling through the desert. They were tired, hot, and thirstier than they had ever been before.

After three days of hiking through the desert with no water, they finally came across a natural pool! They were excited until they tasted it. It was too bitter to drink. Moses prayed to God. He had to find some way to get his followers water! God showed Moses a tree and told him to throw it in the pool. When he did this, the water became clear and sweet. Moses and his people drank happily.

They could not stay by this pool. Moses led them on. They reached a land called Elim. Elim had a beautiful oasis, filled with twelve springs and seventy date trees! The people were happy in Elim. They drank, washed, ate dates, and rested. It was almost like they had found the Garden of Eden. There was just one problem. They could not live on a diet of dates alone.

The Hebrews and eaten all the food they had taken with them from Egypt. Some began to lose hope. At least in Egypt, they had meat to cook, and grains with which to make bread. Some of the people got very angry with Moses for leading them into the desert.

Moses remained brave. He knew that he was doing the work of God. The journey may be hard, but God would provide for His people. Moses continued to pray. God answered, and told Moses that He would make it rain bread. This would be a test for his people. Each day, they were to gather only what they could eat in one day. On the sixth day, what they could gather twice as much as what they could eat in one day.

God promised that he would provide meat for dinner, and in the morning, there would be bread for breakfast.

That evening, the people saw what looked like a huge cloud coming toward them. At first, they were afraid. Then they saw that the cloud was a huge flock of quails! The quails filled the camp, and the Hebrews had a delicious dinner. They went to bed happy, with full bellies.

The next morning, the ground was covered with dew. When the sun burned off the dew, the ground was covered with tiny white flakes. Moses told the people that this was the bread God has promised them. It was called manna. He asked them to gather only as much manna as they could eat that day. But the people were scared. They had been hungry for too long.

Out of fear, some of the people gathered more manna than they could eat that day. The next morning, the leftovers were filled with worms! It had to be thrown out. After that, the people gathered what they could eat each day, and the rest melted as the sun grew hot.

On the sixth day, the people were instructed to gather twice as much manna as they could eat. They were to cook it all that day, but only eat half. The second half was to be saved for the next day when they would celebrate the Sabbath. They were to rest on the Sabbath, not gather any more food. This was to celebrate the seventh day of creation when God rested.

On the seventh day, some people disobeyed and tried to gather manna anyway. There was none of the ground. Moses became angry that the people were still not listening to the instructions he gave them from God. God continued to feed His people manna for forty years, as they wandered through the desert. Finally, they reached the land of Canaan.

The End of the Journey

Forty years was a long time to travel through the desert. The people were tired, hungry, and thirsty. They lost faith that they would ever find a home. More than a home, they wanted water! The Hebrews were so thirsty that Moses even began to fear his own people.

Moses never doubted his faith. He knew God would provide. Moses prayed to God and asked what he should do. Following God's instructions, Moses asked some of the oldest of his people to follow him. He led them to a rock on the mountain of Horeb. Moses hit the rock with his staff. This was the same staff he used to bring on the plagues of Egypt. This time, a good thing happened. Water started to flow from the rock! The people quenched their thirst. Faith was restored.

When Moses left Midian many decades before, his wife Zipporah, and his two sons had moved in with Jethro. Jethro was Zipporah's father and Moses' father-in-law. Jethro had heard about how Moses saved the Hebrews from Egypt, and the wonders that God had performed to help them.

Jethro looked for Moses and found him camping on Mount Sinai. Jethro sent messengers to let Moses know he was coming to see him, and with Zipporah and her two sons. Moses happily went to meet his father-in-law, first bowing to him, then kissing him.

Moses told Jethro about his time in Egypt, and his years wandering in the desert. Jethro told Moses how his wife and two sons were doing. Jethro was very happy to hear how God had saved the Hebrews. Jethro's faith was restored, and he declared,

"Now I know that the Lord is greater than all the gods."

Exodus 18:11

Jethro made offerings and sacrifices to God. He then invited Moses, Aaron, and the Hebrew elders to join him for a meal.

The next day, Jethro saw that Moses spent all day settling disagreements between his people. When he asked why, Moses told him that he was speaking for God, as he alone knew all the rules. Jethro told him this was too much for any person to do. With Jethro's help, Moses selected representatives from his people. He taught them God's rules. The major disputes were still brought to Moses, but the new judges and leaders were able to handle most themselves.

Moses was grateful for Jethro's help. But he could not stay with him forever. He had to lead his people home. They said a fond goodbye, and Moses led his people onwards.

Chapter 17: The Ten Commandments

(Exodus 19-20)

Three months after escaping Egypt, Moses led his followers to Sinai. They set up a camp in front of the mountain. Moses left the camp and climbed the mountain so he could speak to God. Moses heard God tell him that He was ready to tell Moses His laws.

Before God would tell Moses His laws, he and the people had to prepare for three days. God told Moses to remind the people of all the things God had done for them. The people were to wash their clothes. They were not allowed to climb the mountain. They were not allowed to hug or kiss each other.

On the third day, thunder, lightning, and a cloud

filled the morning air. Trumpets sounded and the people were afraid. Moses led his people out of their camp to the foot of the mountain. They were ready to meet God.

The mountain began to quake and the noise of the trumpets grew louder. All of Mount Sinai was surrounded with smoke. When Moses spoke, God answered with claps of thunder. God came to the top of the mountain and called Moses up to him.

God warned Moses that the people should not look directly at Him. Only the priests should come near. Finally, God spoke to all the people, delivering His Ten Commandments.

"You shall have no other gods before Me.

You shall not make for yourself an idol...

You shall not take the name of the Lord your God in vain...

Remember the sabbath day, to keep it holy...

Honor your father and your mother...

You shall not murder.

You shall not commit adultery.

You shall not steal.

You shall not bear false witness against your

neighbor.

You shall not covet your neighbor's house... life...

servant... ox or donkey...

Exodus 20:3-17

Moses left God and went back to his people. Moses told them God had provided them with ten laws that they must obey. As his people listened, still afraid of what they had seen and heard, Moses listed the commandments.

1) God is the only god.
2) Worship nothing and no one, except God.
3) Say God's name with respect.
4) Always rest on the seventh day.

5) Obey and respect your parents.

6) Do not kill anyone.

7) If you are a man, do not try to take another man's wife. If you are a woman, don't try to take another woman's husband.

8) Don't take anything that doesn't belong to you.

9) Always be honest.

10) Do not be jealous of what other people have.

Moses carved these rules onto two large pieces of stones. They were named The Ten Commandments. From this time forward, these were the most important laws to all people who followed God. The people built an ark to carry the stones that had the commandments carved into them. This was much smaller than Noah's ark! This ark was meant to be carried.

Chapter 18: Joshua and the Spies

(Joshua 2)

Moses led a long life, full of travel and adventure. It was not always easy, but it was a great life. He accomplished more than most people could even dream of. Before Moses died, he named Joshua as the next leader of the Hebrews. Moses passed away before he reached the Promised Land. He was too old to go on. He knew that they were close, so he died in peace. He knew his people would eventually reach their true home. Moses had pointed out the way to Joshua.

Joshua selected two men to use as spies. He asked them to go and see the lands around them. He particularly wanted them to report back on the city of Jericho. God wanted the city of

Jericho to be cleansed of evil.

The two spies snuck into the city of Jericho. The King of Jericho heard they were there and was angry. The king sent men out to look for the spies, and capture them. Fortunately, the spies met a woman named Rahab. She had a bad reputation, but a good heart. She helped to hide the spies. When the King of Jericho sent his men to capture the spies, she said that she had seen them, but didn't know where they went.

The men left to find the spies. Rahab went up to her roof. This is where she had hidden the two spies. She brought them food and told them that they were safe.

Rahab had heard all about the Hebrews; how they had escaped the Egyptians, and won many battles on their journey through the desert. In return for Rahab's kindness, the two spies promised that she and her family would be safe if there was a fight over the city of Jericho. If there was ever a fight, they told her that she should hang something red out of her window. That way, they could find her and help her.

After the spies had seen the city, Rahab helped them to leave. Her house was by the wall of the city. From her roof, they were able to use a rope to safely climb over the wall. Rahab instructed the men to hide in the hills for three days. Then they would be able to avoid the army that was looking for them and travel back to their people.

When the spies got back to Joshua, they reported back all of what they had seen. Joshua and his followers started to plan how to take over the city. What God had commanded, they would do.

Chapter 19: The Battle of Jericho

(Joshua 6)

After the spies left, the people of Jericho had strengthened their walls. They were determined to defend their city! The gates were tightly closed. Joshua prayed to God for advice. How would they get into the city?

Joshua was told to lead his army around the city one time. They should do this for six days. During this march, seven priests were to carry trumpets, followed by the ark containing the commandments. On the seventh day, the army was to march around the city walls seven times. During this march, the priests were to blow the trumpets. Everyone should be quiet during these marches, except for the trumpets on the seventh day. Only when Joshua signaled them, should they shout.

Joshua's people thought these instructions were odd. What was the point of quietly marching around the walls? However, for six days, they followed instructions. They walked quietly around the walls once a day then returned to their camp.

On the seventh morning, the army marched around the city walls seven times, while the priests blew their horns. On the seventh time, Joshua yelled to his people, "Shout! God has given you the city!" As the army shouted and the priests blew their trumpets, the walls of Jericho crumbled to the ground!

Joshua's army ran into the city. They won every fight and gathered treasures to give to God. Rahab and her family were not forgotten. Joshua sent the two spies to her home. They helped her pack and brought her and her whole family to safety.

When the city was empty of Joshua's army and Rahab and her family were safe, the whole city was burned down. Joshua then cursed the land in the name of God. Any man who rebuilt the city would do so at great cost to themselves. After this battle, Joshua became famous throughout the land.

Chapter 20: Gideon's Battle

(Judges 6-8)

After Joshua's death, the Hebrews did not have a leader. They tried to obey God's laws, but they faced temptation. They saw other people acting against the laws of God and began to act like them. They knew it was wrong, but temptation became too strong.

For seven years, the Hebrews were overpowered by the people of Midian. The Midianites would harm the Hebrews and steal from them. They stole the food they had grown, their animals, and ruined their fields.

Even though His people had strayed, they had not forgotten God. They called to Him in their time of need. God reminded the people how He saved them from slavery and brought them back to their own lands. He told them He was angry that the people had disobeyed Him.

Despite His anger, God was like any parent. He still loved His children. He would help set them back on the right path. God sent an angel to Gideon, a young Hebrew. The angel told Gideon that he was going to be the one to save his people. Gideon didn't believe it! He was the youngest of all his father's son, and no one paid much attention to him. His family did not have a high rank in the community.

Gideon thought it must be a mistake, and he told the angel so. The angel was sure of his message from God. Gideon asked if the angel would wait while he prepared an offering for God. He hoped that when this offering was given, he would get a sign from God.

Gideon prepared a meal as an offering and returned to the angel. The angel told Gideon to put the meat and bread on a rock. He was then to pour the soup onto the rock. When Gideon did this, a fire started on the rock! The fire ate the meal, and the angel disappeared.

Gideon was confident that he had received a sign from God! He had truly been visited by one of God's angels! Gideon would be the one to save his people from the Midianites! Gideon built an altar dedicated to God on the spot where he had presented the offering.

That night, on God's command, Gideon gathered several of his father's servants and bulls. Together, they tore down the altars his people had created to other gods. When the people awoke in the morning and saw their altars to the gods had been ruined, they were very angry. They started questioning people and soon learned that Gideon is the one who had destroyed the altars.

Joash, Gideon's father, defended his son. Joash told the people to pray to their false gods. He suggested they ask the gods to take their own revenge. The people agreed. Nothing happened to Gideon since there is only one true God.

Gideon began to send out messengers. They were looking for people brave enough to fight the Midianites. Thirty-two thousand people gathered on Mount Gilead. God told Gideon this was too many. He wanted his people to know that God was leading them to victory, not a huge army.

On God's command, Gideon spoke to his army. He told them that anyone who was scared should leave. Twenty-two thousand people left. It was now an army of ten thousand people. God told Gideon this was still too many. God had Gideon test the remaining men.

Following God's orders, Gideon brought his followers to the water to drink. The people who kneeled to drink were sent home. The people who used their hands as cups, from which they lapped, would be the army. After this final test, the army was down to three hundred people.

Gideon and his remaining army packed up their food and weapons. They were ready!

That night, God asked Gideon to take his servant Purah, and walk to the camp of the Midianites and Amalekites; their enemies. The two men obeyed, and they overheard their enemies admit they were afraid. One man was telling his friend about a dream he'd had. In the man's dream, a loaf of bread was tumbling through their camp, and when it hit a tent, the tent fell over! The man's friend interpreted the dream. He said that it meant God had given Gideon the Midianite their camp.

Gideon happily returned to camp and announced to his army that God was going to give them the Midianites' camp. Gideon divided his army into three groups. Everyone was given trumpets and pitchers covering lit torches. The army was instructed to surround the Midianites' camp. When Gideon blew the trumpet, the army should blow theirs, and yell, "For God and for Gideon!"

Gideon led his army into place. Gideon blew his trumpet, and so did his followers. They all broke their pitchers, lighting up the night with their torches. They shouted, "A sword for God and for Gideon!"

The three hundred trumpets blared and the torches lit up the night. In the confusion of sound and sudden light, the Midianites began to fight against each other! They fought themselves and ran away in fear. With God's help, Gideon and his people won the battle, without having to do any violence!

Chapter 21: Samson and Delilah

(Judges 13-16)

A man lived in Israel by the name of Manoah. He and his wife were unable to have children. They prayed to God that he would bless them with a child. One day, an angel came to visit Manoah's wife. The angel promised her that she would have a son!

Manoah was thrilled to hear this news. He prayed to send the angel back. He wanted to ask the angel how he should raise his son. He wanted to make sure that he was a good father!

When the angel returned, he told Manoah and his wife that they must raise their son to serve God. Their son would grow to be very big and strong. He should never drink alcohol, and should always eat healthy food. To show that he was dedicated to God, his hair should never be cut.

When Manoah and his wife were finally blessed with a child, they named him Samson.

Samson was a Nazarite who was known throughout the lands as being much bigger and stronger than all other men. A Nazarite is someone who took a vow to be dedicated to God.

Although Samson's parents had promised he would always serve God, Samson sometimes had trouble following that promise. He was brave and was always ready to help someone defend themselves against their enemies. But he also had a temper and tended to be more violent than he needed to be. This was not always his fault. His strength was hard to control.

Samson fell in love with a Philistine woman named Timnath. He even killed a lion to protect her. He married her and threw a feast as a celebration. During the celebration, he challenged men with a riddle he thought they could never figure out. Timnath made the mistake of telling the men the answer to the riddle.

In a fit of rage, Samson stormed out of the house. He felt betrayed. By the time he came to his senses, the Philistines had taken Timnath and married her off to another man. Samson was devastated. He traveled the land to try and forget about the wife he had lost with his temper.

When Samson was in the city of Gaza, there were men plotting to hurt him. Samson heard about this plot, so he escaped the city by pulling up the gates, and carrying them up a mountain!

Although Samson missed his wife, he never he would never get her back. Eventually, he fell in love again with a woman named Delilah. She was a Philistine woman who lived in the valley of Sorek. Samson was a good man, but this did not mean that he had good taste in women. The leaders of the Philistines told Delilah to find out where Samson got all his strength. If she succeeds, she would be very well paid in silver!

Delilah asked Samson to show her where he got his strength. Even though he loved her, Samson did not trust Delilah enough to tell the truth. Samson claimed that if he was tied by seven ropes, that were still green, and not yet dried, he would lose his strength.

Delilah told the Philistine leaders that she had succeeded in finding Samson's secret! That night, they hid in the house. When Samson fell asleep, she used seven green ropes and tied him up. Delilah yelled, pretending to warn Samson that the Philistines were coming to get him. He awoke and easily broke the ropes.

Delilah pretended to be sad that Samson had lied to her. But she was really just sad that she had not gotten paid! Delilah asked again where

Samson got his strength. This time, Samson said that ropes that had not been used on anyone else would take away his strength.

Delilah reported to the Philistine leaders, and they hid in her house. Once Samson was sleep, she tied him up, using a rope that hadn't been used on anyone else. When she was done, Delilah shouted, "The Philistines are here to get you, Samson!" Samson sat up, breaking the ropes that bound him with ease.

Not one to give up easily, Delilah pouted, insisting that Samson tell her how his strength could be controlled. This time, Samson told her that if his hair was divided into seven sections, braided with a loom, and secured with a pin, he would become as weak as a normal man.

That night, Delilah and the Philistines tried again. Then men hid while Samson slept, and Delilah braided his hair. When Delilah shouted her warning, Samson leaped out of bed, easily pulling himself free with very little effort.

Delilah was determined to get paid. She wept to Samson. Delilah told Samson how much she loved him, and how sad she was that he would not tell her the truth. She begged every day to learn the truth. Finally, Samson could stand it no longer. He admitted to Delilah that his hair had never been cut. It was to show that he was a Nazarite who had been promised to God. That is why he was so strong. Cutting his hair would make him as weak as a regular man.

Delilah had a feeling Samson had finally told her the truth. She reported to the leaders of the Philistines. That night, the Philistines came, bringing the silver Delilah had been promised. When Samson fell asleep, she quietly called over a man with a razor. The man shaved off all of Samson's hair.

Like the times before, Delilah called a warning, "The Philistines are upon you, Samson!" Samson awoke, not realizing that his strength was gone. The Philistines grabbed him. They took out his eyes, and tied him up, and took him to prison. Samson no longer had the strength to break the ropes that held him.

The Philistines were cruel and sneaky, but they were not very smart. They forgot that hair grows. While Samson was stuck in prison, his hair grew, as did his strength!

The Philistines were planning a celebration for their god, Dagon. The thought it would be funny to have Samson at the celebration. They were showing off that they had captured the biggest and strongest man in the world. To show how weak Samson now was, they had a young boy lead him. Samson asked the boy if he could lean on the pillars.

While three thousand Philistines were being amused by Samson's fate, his faith in God remained strong. Samson prayed that God would remember him and give him back his full strength just this one last time. He asked to be able to punish the evil men that took his eyes. Samson no longer cared for his own life.

God granted Samson his last wish. Samson pushed on the pillars, and the whole building came tumbling down. Samson was crushed, along with the Philistines. With his death, Samson killed more evil men than he had killed in his whole lifetime of doing battle. Samson's family was able to take his body, and he was buried at home.

Samson's death is very sad, but it put an end to his suffering. God allowed him to avenge himself in his last moments, and rid the world of thousands of wicked people. It was an end any warrior could be proud of.

Chapter 22: Naomi and Ruth

(Ruth 1-5)

Elimelech traveled with his wife Naomi, and their two sons, Mahlon and Chilion, to the land of Moab. After they had settled down in Moab, Elimelech passed away. Naomi was very sad, but she had her two sons to comfort her. Mahlon and Chilion met and married two Moabite women; Orpah and Ruth. They all lived together happily for ten years.

Sadly, Mahlon and Chilion both passed away. Naomi was filled with grief. Now that she had lost her husband and two sons, Naomi decided that she would be happier if she moved back to Israel. She may have lost her family, but she could at least be with her own people.

Orpah and Ruth helped Naomi along her travels back to Israel. Along the way, Naomi kissed the young women and told them she loved them. Naomi blessed Orpah and Ruth for helping her begin her journey. Thanking them for all they had done for her, Naomi told the young women to return to their homeland. They could move back in with their parents. Naomi had nothing left to give them. She wished she could provide them with more sons to marry, but she was too old. She did not expect to get married again, so would have no more children.

Orpah said a tearful goodbye and left her mother-and-sister-in-law. Ruth refused to leave Naomi. She hugged her tight and would not let go. Naomi urged Ruth to follow Orpah. Ruth held tight and promised Naomi,

"Where you go, I will go, and where you lodge, I will lodge. Your people shall be my people, and your God, my God."

Ruth 1:16

Naomi saw that she could not change Ruth's mind and gratefully accepted her company. She loved her daughter-in-law as if she was her true daughter. The two women continued on to Bethlehem.

When Naomi reached Bethlehem, she was greeted by all the people she had known before. She was thankful to be home but was still sad for the loss of her husband and sons.

The women arrived in Bethlehem just as the barley harvest was beginning. At this time, it was legal for poor people to collect scraps of grain left behind during a harvest. Ruth asked Naomi for permission to go and collect some grain, and

Naomi said yes.

While she was collecting grain, Ruth met Boaz. He was the wealthy owner of the fields, and it turned out he was Elimelech's cousin! Boaz was also a very kind man. Boaz told Ruth that she should stay in his fields, collecting grain. He told her to follow the other girls and offered her water.

Ruth asked Boaz why he was being so nice to a stranger. Boaz explained that he had heard that his cousin and his sons had passed away. He had also learned of Naomi's return. He had learned of Ruth's kindness in staying with her mother-in-law. As Ruth tried to thank him for his generosity, he invited Ruth to eat with his other workers at lunch.

After lunch, Ruth headed back out to the fields. Boaz instructed his workers to be nice to Ruth. They were not to say anything unkind. He even asked them to drop some large handfuls of plump grains for her to pick up. When she was thirsty, they should share their water.

That evening, Naomi was shocked by how much grain Ruth had gathered! Naomi blessed the kindness of whoever had helped Ruth. Naomi was very happy when Ruth explained how she had met Boaz, and the kindness he had shown her. Naomi thanked God for blessing her with such a kind relative.

Ruth continued to go to Boaz's fields to collect grain through the long harvest season. She and Naomi ate well this whole time. Boaz saw how hard Ruth worked to feed her mother-in-law. He was impressed by her kindness and loyalty. Boaz could not help but fall in love with her!

Boaz wanted to marry Ruth. There was just one problem. Ruth was the widow of Boaz's cousin's son. There was another cousin in Bethlehem that was an even closer relative than Boaz. Legally, this gave the other cousin the first right to marry

Ruth. Naomi had a piece of land owned by Elimelech to sell. The closest cousin had the first right to buy it. Marriage to Ruth would come with the land.

Boaz asked ten leaders of Bethlehem to meet with him. His cousin and rival for Ruth were also there. Boaz asked his cousin if he wanted to buy the land. His cousin replied that he did. Boaz reminded his cousin that if he bought the land, he would also have to marry Ruth.

Boaz's cousin changed his mind. He wanted the land, but he wasn't ready to get married yet! Boaz happily announced to the leaders of the city that they had seen the other cousin refuse his rights to buy the land and marry Ruth. He announced his plans to buy the land and marry Ruth. The elders accepted and blessed this announcement.

Boaz and Ruth joyfully married. Ruth now considered Naomi her mother. Naomi moved in with Ruth and Boaz. They soon blessed her with a grandson, named Obed. The women of Bethlehem saw how close Naomi and Ruth were. They could see how happy it made Ruth in helping taking care of her grandson.

"May he also be to you a restorer of life and a sustainer of your old age; for your daughter-in-law, who loves you and is better to you than seven sons, has given birth to him."

Ruth 4:14-15

Chapter 23: A Voice in the Night

(1 Samuel 1-3)

Elkanah married two women; Peninnah and Hannah. Peninnah gave him children, but Hannah could not. Elkanah still loved Hannah, but Peninnah was often mean to her. Peninnah would brag about her own children while making fun of Hannah for not being able to have any of her own.

Hannah wanted a baby more than anything else in the world. Every year, Elkanah would travel to a temple in Shiloh, where he would worship God, and make sacrifices to Him. Elkanah would give portions of the sacrificed animals to his wives and Peninnah's children, but Hannah cried too much and was not able to eat.

One night, while praying at the temple, Hannah promised God that He allowed her to have a baby, she would put him in the service of God for his entire life. A priest named Eli saw her pray.

Since Hannah was so upset, she was practically hysterical, he thought she'd just had too much wine! Hannah explained to Eli that she was simply sad and praying for a baby. Eli promised her God would answer her prayers.

The next morning, the family worshipped God one last time at the temple, then headed home to Ramah. Soon, Hannah gave birth to a baby boy! Hannah was filled with joy. She named him Samuel.

When Elkanah went to the temple for his yearly visit, Hannah did not join him. She said that she would not return until Samuel was finished nursing.

When Samuel was old enough, Hannah brought

him up to the temple. She took with her a young bull, flour, and wine. Eli did not recognize Hannah, but she reminded him who she was, and proudly introduced him to her son, Samuel. Hannah explained that she was ready to fulfill her end of the bargain with God. Samuel would enter the service of the Lord. His service would begin by helping Eli.

Although Hannah was sad to say goodbye to Samuel, she was very thankful that she'd had him. She sang a song of thanks and praise to the Lord.

"The Lord makes poor and rich;
He brings low, He also exalts.
He raises the poor from the dust,
He lifts the needy from the ash heap
To make them sit with nobles,
And inherit a seat of honor."
1 Samuel 2:7-8

Eli was very happy to have young Samuel to help him. Eli was very old, and going blind, so help was a blessing. Samuel was a good boy, and Eli's sons were bad! Eli's sons did not follow God. When people were making sacrifices to God, they would steal the sacrificed! They did many other wicked things as well, to God, and to other people.

Men came to Eli to tell him how badly his sons were acting. They told Eli about his sins against other people, and even worse, their sins against God. Eli was a good man, but not a brave man. He told his sons to end their wicked ways but did not stop them. He did not want to leave the temple and was not able to control them.

Every year, when Elkanah brought his family to the temple to worship, they were very happy to get to visit with Samuel. Each year, Hannah brought him a new robe that she had made. To show how thankful he was to have Samuel, Eli would give Elkanah and Hannah a special blessing.

"May the Lord give you children from this woman in the place of the one she dedicated to the Lord.

1 Samuel 2:20

Hannah and Elkanah were blessed with three more sons and two daughters! The mean-spirited Penninah could taunt Hannah no longer. Hannah was very happy with her husband and children, but she did forget about Samuel. She loved him deeply and thought about him every day.

Samuel was growing into a wonderful young man. He was favored by God, and well-liked by all the men who knew him. One evening, Samuel and Eli were lying down in their tent. Samuel heard a voice call his name. "Samuel!" Samuel got out of bed and went to Eli. Samuel asked Eli why he had been called. Was something wrong? Eli said that he had not called Samuel, and told him to go bad to bed.

A voice called out "Samuel!" again. Again, Samuel climbed out of bed and went to check on Eli. Again, Eli told Samuel that he had not said anything, and sent him back to bed. The third time this happened, Eli realized what was happening. God was speaking to Eli! By this time, visits from God were rare. This is why it took three times for Eli to realize what was happening.

Eli explained to Samuel that God was speaking to him. Samuel's faith in God and his respect for Eli was so strong that he believed him immediately. Eli told Samuel that if God called again, Samuel should answer, and tell Him that he was listening. When God called Samuel for the third time, Samuel answered according to Eli's instructions.

God told Samuel that he was going to end Eli's line. Eli's sons would have no sons. There would be no more descendants of the family line. God was doing this because Eli's sons were sinners, who were not sorry. This was also a punishment for Eli. Eli was a good man and dedicated to God, but he had not done enough in his efforts to stop his sons' wicked behavior.

The next morning, Eli asked if God had spoken to Samuel again. Samuel did not want to tell Eli what God had told him. Samuel respected and cared greatly for Eli, and did not want to hurt his feelings. Eli asked Samuel to tell him the truth. Samuel did, and Eli accepted the news calmly. Eli trusted that God knew what was good and right.

As Samuel grew older, he became known as a prophet of God throughout the lands.

Throughout Samuel's life, God continued to visit him and speak to him.

Chapter 24: Israel's First King

(1 Samuel 8-10)

God Warns Samuel

I srael is the homeland of the Hebrew people. The people wanted a king to rule their country. Samuel, the prophet, was known as the wisest person in the land. People listened to him and came to him for advice because they knew God spoke to him.

As Samuel grew old, he picked his two sons, to be leaders in Israel. Sadly, Joel and Abijah were more like Eli's sons than their own father. They did not follow God. They accepted bribes and were not fair leaders.

The people of Israel saw that Joel and Abijah

were not good leaders. The people came to Samuel and told him his sons were bad leaders. They asked Samuel to choose a king.

Samuel prayed to God and asked Him to guide him. God was angry that the people wanted to worship a king. God had done so much for His people since He helped them escape Egypt. Now they were turning away from Him again. God asked Samuel to explain to his people the dangers of having a king that would rule over them.

"Listen to the voice of the people in regard to all that they say to you, for they have not rejected you, but they have rejected Me from being king over them. Like all the deeds which they have done since the day I brought them up from Egypt even to this day; they have forsaken Me and served other gods."

1 Samuel 8:7-8

Samuel spoke to the people. He explained that a king would just take for himself and his family. A king would take the best food grown in the fields, the best animals to work in his own fields. A king would take the best servants for his own. He would take people's daughters to work in his palace.

The people did not listen to God's words spoken through Samuel. They wanted a king so that they could be like other countries. They wanted a king that would lead them in war, and help them win battles.

God told Samuel to do what the people asked. Pick a king for them. But when the king was not fair, they should not expect God to save them. He had warned them of the danger.

Saul's Search

Saul was the tallest, most handsome man in all of the land called Benjamin. Saul was also a good person. Everyone who knew Saul liked him. They thought he had a bright future. Saul's father, Kish, had lost all of his donkeys. Kish told Saul to go find his donkeys. Saul was allowed to take one of his father's servants to help him.

Saul and his servant traveled through many lands looking for the lost donkeys. Once they reached Zuph, Saul decided it was time to go home. By now, Kish would be more worried about him than the donkeys. The servant told Saul about a wise man he had heard of. This man, known as a prophet, would be able to give them advice on their journey. They could ask the prophet where they could find the lost donkeys and the best way to get home.

Saul and his servant traveled on to the city where the prophet lived. As they got near to the city, they saw three women by a well. They asked the women if the prophet was in the city. They answered that the prophet was there, but leaving soon. He was going to climb into the mountains to pray and sacrifice for God.

Taking the women's advice, Saul and his servant hurried towards the city. As they were entering the city, met Samuel the prophet as he was leaving!

God Sends a King

The day before Saul and his servant got to the city, God had spoken with Samuel. God told Samuel that He would send a man from Benjamin, who Samuel should select as King of Israel.

When Samuel saw Saul, God said, "That is him, the future King of Israel!" When Saul and Samuel reached each other, Saul asked for directions to the prophet. Samuel responded that he was the prophet, and invited Saul to come along with him to eat, worship, and sacrifice. The next morning, Saul could leave.

Before Saul could ask about his lost donkeys, Samuel told him they had been found. Saul should no longer worry about the donkeys, Samuel had a much more important task for him.

When Samuel brought to Saul to dine, he seated him at the head of the table. Saul was given a special portion of food.

Saul was not used to being treated with respect. Saul was from Benjamin, the smallest tribe in the land. Saul's family had the lowest rank in this smallest of tribes.

The next morning, Samuel got Saul up early. Samuel took Saul to the edge of the city. When they passed through the gates, Samuel took from his pockets a bottle of oil and poured it over Saul's head. Samuel then kissed Saul. Samuel explained to Saul that God had selected Saul as the next leader of His people.

God, through Samuel, gave Saul instructions for his journey. Saul was told to go to find two men that would be bear Rachel's tomb. These men would tell Saul that Kish's donkeys had been found. Kish was no longer worried about his donkeys, just his son. After this, Saul was to walk to Mount Tabor, where he would meet three men. One man would be carrying three children, the other three loaves a bread, and the third, a bottle of wine. These men would greet Saul, and give him two loaves of bread.

Finally, Samuel told Saul that he should continue his journey to the hill of God. The Philistines were gathered there. As Saul walked down from the hill to the city, he would meet a group of prophets who were playing instruments and speaking the word of God. When with these men, Saul would also speak the word of God, and be a changed man.

Samuel told Saul that if these things happened, it

meant that he was truly picked by God to be king. In seven days, Samuel would come to Saul to help him rule.

Saul left Samuel and began his travels. As instructed, he went to Rachel's tomb, Mount Tabor, and the hill of God. Everything happened just like Samuel said it would!

As promised, Samuel joined Saul on the seventh day. He called all the people together, and announced that Saul was their king, selected by God! Most people were happy, they wanted a king, and God provided them with one.

Some people of Israel were upset. They did not think that Saul was important enough to be king. They judged him on where he was from, and who is family was. These people did not bring gifts to their new king, or celebrate his rule. Saul did not punish any of these people.

Chapter 25: David and Goliath

(1 Samuel 17)

The Philistines and Israelites were camped on two mountains, with a valley between them. They were preparing to battle each other. Goliath was a giant Philistine. He was ten feet tall and was wore a bronze helmet and armor. Goliath carried a huge spear. He was such an important warrior that he had someone to carry his shield for him.

Goliath was a violent man who loved to fight. He was known across the lands for being unbeatable. The sight of him struck fear in the hearts of his enemies. Goliath yelled across the valley to the group of Israelites and challenged them to fight him. Goliath was so impressed with his own skills that he said that if an Israelite fought him and won, the Philistines would be servants to the Israelites. But, if Goliath won the fight, all the Israelites would be servants to the Philistines.

The Israelites were led by King Saul. They were all scared, even the king. Goliath shouted the same challenge every day. No one was brave enough to fight him. This continued for forty days! King Saul offered a prize to whoever could beat Goliath. The victor would be presented with riches, and be allowed to marry Saul's daughter!

Jesse had four sons. Three were in the army, but David, the youngest, was still at home. David was busy taking care of the sheep and caring for his elderly father. One day, Jesse packed up some food for his three oldest sons. He told David to take this food to his brothers and see how the battle was going.

The next morning, David took the food Jesse had packed and started his walk to the mountain.

When David was giving the food to his brothers, he heard Goliath's challenge. David was curious about the giant man. He found out that the person who beat Goliath would be rewarded with treasure, and get to marry the daughter of the king.

David was young, but he was very brave. David decided to accept Goliath's challenge. The soldiers brought David to King Saul. David was confident that he could bet Goliath. King Saul doubted David. He was too young, much too inexperienced! Goliath had fought and killed many men before David was even born.

David was determined. He told King Saul that even though he was a shepherd, not a soldier, he was ready for battle. When taking care of his sheep, David had fought off bears and lions. He could certainly fight this giant. David had God on his side, Goliath did not. David's faith made him sure that God would take care of him during his fight with Goliath.

King Saul gave in to David. He was not confident that David would win, but no one else was brave enough to volunteer. King Saul asked God to watch over David during his fight. The king even gave David his own armor to use.

When David put on King Saul's armor, it was too heavy. He could barely move in it. David took off the armor and picked five stones from the river. David would face Goliath with just these stones, a stick, and a sling.

Goliath laughed as David walked up to him. He was barely an adult! Goliath thought it was funny that David brought sticks to battle. "Am I a dog?" he yelled. David responded that while Goliath had weapons, David had God on his side.

The fight began as Goliath started coming towards David, with his weapons raised. David selected one of his stones, put it in his sling, and aimed. David's aim was true. He hit Goliath right in the middle of his forehead! Goliath slowly fell to the ground with a mighty crash. He did not rise again.

David approached the fallen giant. He took Goliath's sword and removed his head. The Philistines were terrified. How did this shepherd boy beat their fearless warrior? They turn and ran away. As they ran, they heard the Israelites' shouts of victory.

Chapter 26: The Friendship of David and Jonathan

(1 Samuel 18-20)

King Saul's Court

After David beat Goliath, he was invited to live at King Saul's court, as part of his prize. At court, David quickly made a new friend; Jonathan, Saul's son. David and Jonathan loved each other like they were brothers. As a prince, Jonathan had everything he could want. He was happy to share everything with his new friend.

As the man who had beaten the giant Goliath, David was frequently sent by Saul into battle. David was a handsome man. This, along with his victories in battle made him very popular with the women in the king's court. When David returned, the women would dance, play musical instruments, and sing,

---

> "Saul has slain his thousands,
> And David his ten thousand."
>
> **1 Samuel 18:7**

This made King Saul very jealous. He was king, but David was far more admired. One day, Saul could stand his jealousy no longer. While David was playing the harp, Saul threw a spear at him! Luckily, the spear missed David. King Saul became increasingly angry at David, and he even became afraid. King Saul did not know why David was so loved by God, while it seemed He had forgotten the king.

King Saul put David in charge of an army of one thousand men. This was not out of kindness, or appreciation, but out of fear. King Saul wanted

David far away in battle, not in his court. King Saul hoped that David would not return from battle. However, David continually led his army to victory. He became increasingly loved and respected throughout the land.

King Saul saw that his plan was backfiring. He continued to plot against David. King Saul promised David that he could marry Merab, his oldest daughter. All David had to do was go into battle and kill one hundred Philistines. King Saul hoped that David would be beaten, and be unable to return from battle.

David returned home safely once again. He had done what King Saul had asked. But, King Saul had betrayed David. He had already given his daughter Merab to Adriel.

Michal, King's Saul's other daughter, was in love with David. Michal confessed her feelings to her father. King Saul promised Michal to David. There was a catch. David had to kill one hundred more Philistines.

King Saul's plan failed again. David returned home from battle safely. Not only had he done what King Saul had demanded, but he had also doubled it! This time, King Saul kept his promise. Michal and David were married. King Saul became even angrier at David. Not only did God love him best, but so did King Saul's own daughter.

King Saul was tired of plotting in secret. It was not getting him anywhere. He admitted to his servants and his son, Jonathan, that he wanted to kill David! Jonathan was very upset. He loved his father, but David was his best friend. They were like brothers!

Jonathan went against his own father to warn his dear friend. Jonathan told David that King Saul was planning to kill him. The two friends started planning immediately. The next morning, David would get up early and hide. Jonathan would walk with his father into the fields, and see if he could get any more information.

Jonathan tried to reason with his father. He reminded King Saul of David's brave acts, and how much he had helped the people of Israel. David had never done anything to hurt the king. Jonathan's words deeply affected King Saul. He was sorry about how he had acted towards David. King Saul promised Jonathan that his best friend would not be harmed. Jonathan was excited to tell David he could safely return home.

Peace did not last for long in these times. David was soon sent back out to war. David returned home victoriously. Unfortunately, this was too much for King Saul. Evil entered his heart, and while David played the harp, the king threw a spear at him. The king's aim was off, and David escaped unharmed.

That night, Michal encouraged her husband to run away. She did not want him to leave, but this was the only way to save his life. Before he left, David put a quilt in his bed, under the linens. Michal helped him to fold the quilt to resemble the shape of a human. They hoped this would trick anyone who tried to harm David in the night. When the preparations were complete, Michal helped David to climb out the window. They knew that the king had sent spies to watch their house.

King Saul sent his spies into the house with orders to bring David to him. They were fooled by the quilt that was stuffed under the bed linens. The spies reported to Saul that David was sick in bed. The king himself went to the house, threw back the covers, and saw that he had been tricked. King Saul was very angry with his daughter for helping his enemy.

On the Run

After David's escape, he traveled to Ramah. There, he met the prophet, Samuel. David told the prophet about how badly he had been treated by King Saul. Samuel took David to Naioth, where he helped him stay hidden. King Saul sent messengers to Ramah three times with orders to find David and bring him back to the king. Each time they were unsuccessful.

King Saul decided it was time to take charge. He traveled to Ramah. The king asked many people where Samuel and David were. Finally, someone told him that they were hiding in Naioth. Hearing that the king on his trail, David fled. King Saul pretended that he had forgiven David, and sent messengers to spread the word that David could safely return home.

David and Jonathan were able to meet once again. This time, Jonathan did not know that King Saul was plotting against David. But, when David described the recent events to him, Jonathan believed his friend. Jonathan promised David that he would help in any way he could.

The two friends made a plan, based on the feast the next day.

David and Jonathan decided that David would not attend the feast of the new moon. If King Saul asked where David was, Jonathan would tell his father that David had returned to his childhood home in Bethlehem. If Saul was not upset by this news, they would know that the king's claim was true; David would be safe. If King Saul got angry, they would know the king still planning to harm David.

According to the plan, during the feast, King Saul asked Jonathan why David was not in his seat. Jonathan responded that his friend had returned to Bethlehem. King Saul could not contain his rage. He yelled at Jonathan, telling him that his friendship with David would ruin his life. Jonathan was next in line to be king, but King Saul said that would never happen as long as David lived.

King Saul shouted to his servants that they should go find David so that he could put him to death! Jonathan responded angrily, asking his father why he would kill someone who had been a loyal soldier to him, and never hurt anyone except their enemy.

King Saul exploded with rage. This time, he threw his spear at his own son! Jonathan walked out on his father at his feast. For two days, Jonathan was too worried about his friend and too angry with his father to even eat!

When Jonathan had calmed down, he was able to think logically. He had to warn David! King Saul had been lying, and wanted David put to death more than ever. The friends had a plan to meet after three days in the field. They had a signal worked out.

Following their plan, Jonathan took a young servant boy with him into the fields. Jonathan shot his bow and arrow and told the boy to run and get his arrow. As the boy ran, Jonathan encouraged him to hurry and to run farther and faster. This was his signal to David that it would not be safe to return. King Saul still wanted him dead.

As the servant boy ran through the fields, Jonathan could not resist the chance to say goodbye to his friend. The hugged each other and cried. They promised each other that even though they might never see each other again, they would always be best friends, and pray for each other.

Chapter 27: David Becomes King

(1 Samuel 21 - 2 Samuel 2)

On the Run Again

After David left King Saul's court, he traveled to the holy land of Nob. There, he met a priest named Ahimelech. The priest could tell that something had gone seriously wrong in David's life, and was very nervous around him. He did not want David to stay in Nob. Too afraid of being found by King Saul's men, David did not feel comfortable enough to tell his story to Ahimelech. He did not know whose side Ahimelech would be on.

David pretended that he was there in Nob on King Saul's orders. He asked Ahimelech for bread. David told the priest that he was in such a hurry to leave, that he didn't have time to pack his weapons. Ahimelech told David the only sword he had was the sword of Goliath. This sword was one of a kind! David took the sword and left Nob. Ahimelech was relieved to see him go.

David was not safe in any land that was under the rule of King Saul. He traveled on to the land of Gath. This land was ruled by King Achish. The people of Gath thought it was not smart of the king to let a man like David, who had won so many battles stay in the country. When David heard this, he was afraid King Achish might try to kill him!

David wandered the city of Achish aimlessly, pretending like he had lost his mind. He drooled, talked nonsense to himself, and doodled on walls. He did not want to appear like a threat to the king. The king did not view David as a threat but grew tired of his odd behavior. David was soon thrown out of Gath.

David and His Followers

Giving up on cities, David headed for the wilderness. He found the cave of Adullam and rested there. The cave of Adullam was near his hometown of Bethlehem. David's brothers were happy to hear that he was so close by. They quickly traveled to the cave to visit him. Slowly, more people arrived. People who were in debt or unhappy came. David became the leader of four hundred men.

David's parents were too old to live in a cave, but he wanted to make sure that they were safe. David took his parents to Moab and asked the king if his parents could stay there. The king gave his permission. David's parents were welcome to stay in Moab. David said a tearful goodbye and then went back to the cave and his followers.

One day, Gad, a prophet, came to visit David. Gad advised David to leave the cave and go to Judah. David took his men, and they traveled to the first of Hereth in Judah.

King Saul heard rumors that David was in the forest of Hereth. He gathered his army and continued his hunt. A couple times, King Saul got very close to David, and he barely escaped. Jonathan still traveled with his father. One time, Jonathan was able to sneak away and see David! Jonathan encouraged David to keep going. He told David that King Saul would never catch him. Jonathan may be next in line, but he insisted that David was the one who was destined to be king one day! Jonathan and David promised each other that they would always be friends.

King Saul kept chasing David. One night, unknown to King Saul, they were camping in the same cave! David's followers tried to get him to kill the king. David refused. That night, David crept through the cave while King Saul was sleeping, and cut off a piece of his robe. David was unwilling to harm the king who had been selected by God!

The next morning, when King Saul was a safe distance away, David yelled at him. He held up the piece of the robe he had cut, to show that although he had the chance, he did not harm King Saul.

At this, King Saul realized what he had done. He had spent years of his life trying to harm a man that had never harmed him. David had only been good to King Saul and his family. King Saul finally realized that David was not his enemy.

"You have declared today that you have done good to me, that the Lord delivered me into your hand and yet you did not kill me. For if a man finds his enemy, will he let him go away safely?

May the Lord, therefore, reward you with a good
return for what you have done to me this day."

1 Samuel 24:18-19

King Saul continued to bless David and told him
that David would be king one day. David made
promises to King Saul that he would be kind to
all of the king's family. They would never be
punished for the way King Saul had treated
David.

King Saul returned home, but David returned to
the wilderness. He was thankful that the king
was no longer hunting him, but was too smart to
trust him. The king was known for his sudden
change of temper. No one had more experience
with this than David! David and his followers
stayed in the hills. The viewed David as their
leader, but they did not answer to a king. They
were considered outlaws.

David was right not to trust King Saul. Instead of remembering how David had spared his life, he remembered his own hatred. King Saul and his men began to look for David again.

David's men found King Saul first; they had remained on the lookout. One night, David snuck into the king's tent. Although his followers tried to persuade David to kill the king, David refused. Instead, and took Saul's spear and a flask of water.

When David was a safe distance away, he yelled to Abner, the leader of King Saul's guards. He asked why Abner had not been guarding the king. As proof, that he had been close, but once again spared the king, David told Abner to look for the king's spear and flask.

King Saul woke up when he heard David's voice. When the king realized that David had the chance to harm him, but had chosen not to, he felt very guilty. The king apologized to David and blessed him in the name of God. The two groups parted peacefully.

David was too smart to trust King Saul. He had seen his temper tantrums and sudden changes of moods way too often. He would have considered himself lucky, but he knew that God had been watching over him and protecting him. David decided that he was not safe in Israel. He decided to lead his followers to the land of the Philistines.

King Saul became angry once more. He sent out messengers to track David. When the news reached the king that David had left Israel, King Saul finally stopped looking for him.

David and his followers traveled through the lands of the Philistines, battling people who did not believe in God. They destroyed many Godless cities, taking their livestock and possessions for themselves.

King Saul was eventually killed in a battle against

the Philistines. He ended up falling on his own sword. He was not killed by David, as the king had feared for so many years. Jonathan and two more of King Saul's sons were killed in this battle.

When David heard the news, he was heartbroken. He mourned for the loss of his best friend. David even grieved for King Saul, whom he had once loved. David sang to express his grief.

"Saul and Jonathan, beloved and pleasant in their life,
And in their death, they were not parted;
They were swifter than eagles,
They were stronger than lions....
How have the mighty fallen in the midst of the battle"
2 Samuel 1:23,25

After Saul's death, Abner tried to make Saul's son Ishbosheth king. This was not a popular idea. The people did not like Abner or Ishbosheth. The people wanted to follow David. They had heard of his travels through the Philistine lands. They were impressed by his success in battles.

The people were also impressed by his forgiveness and the mercy he had shown. Although he was ruthless in battle, David repeatedly refused to harm his king, despite the repeated attempts on his own life.

God allowed David time to mourn, but then told him to go to Hebron, a city in the land of Judah. He brought his wives Ahinoam and Abigail, and his followers. The leaders of Judah came to David. He was made a king.

Chapter 28: Solomon Builds a Temple

(1 Kings 6-8)

After King David passed away, his son Solomon became king. God was very important to King Solomon, and he would pray a lot, asking Him to guide him. King David had always wanted to build a temple to God. King Solomon wanted to see his father's greatest wish come true.

King Solomon decided to build the temple on the top of a hill called Zion. The temple was built with stone from a quarry. King Solomon hired the most talented builders to construct the temple. No banging of tools was ever heard during the building of the temple, it was completed in silence.

When the stone temple was built, King Solomon had the workers cover it with cedar planks of wood. The room in the center of the temple was covered in cedar planks, which were then covered in gold. This room would hold the ark. The ark held the Ten Commandments that Moses had carved into stone.

God was pleased with the progress being made on the temple. God spoke to Solomon, promising that as long as Solomon followed His commandments, God would live among the people of Israel. He would watch over them, take care of them, and never leave them.

When the temple was finished, no stone could be seen. It was completely covered with cedar. Most of this wood featured beautiful carvings of angels, plants, and flowers.

In the room where the commandments were going to be held, two angels were carved from the wood of an olive tree. The wings were spread so wide that they touched each other, as well as the walls of the room. These carvings were also covered in gold.

The temple took seven years to build. When it was completed, King Solomon invited all the most important people in Israel to celebrate the ark being placed in the temple. The priests carried the ark into the temple, along with other holy objects. The ark was placed under the wings of the angels, covering and protecting it.

When the ark was placed, God filled the temple with a thick cloud. In response, Solomon said to the people and to God,

---

"The Lord has said that He would dwell in a thick cloud.
I have surely built You a lofty house,
A place for Your dwelling forever!"
1 Kings 8:12-13

King Solomon continued. He explained that he was not trying to shut God into a room. The temple would be a place that people could come to worship God. The beauty of the temple would remind them of God's glory.

With the temple complete, King Solomon's people grew even more confident in his rule. He was showing himself to be a wise man, who would lead them according to the path God set up for them.

Chapter 29: King Ahab and Elijah

(1 Kings 17-18)

Elijah's Prophecy

After the rule of King Solomon, his kingdom was split in two. Israel was ruled by one king, and Judah by another. King Ahab ruled Israel. He was not a good king. He worshipped the false god, Baal, and did many wicked things. He did not have God in his life.

One day, an old man came to see King Ahab. The prophet, named Elijah, gave King Ahab a message from God. Elijah told King Ahab that there would not be any rain in the land unless God willed it. There would not even be morning dew. This would cause a drought. A drought happens when there is not enough water for people to drink, or water their fields, for a long period of time. It is very dangerous!

Elijah was scared of King Ahab. The king was very angry with Elijah. God understood this, so He told Elijah to travel east of the land of Jordan. Here, Elijah would find a small stream that he could drink from. God would tell the ravens that lived there to bring Elijah breakfast and dinner each day.

Elijah obeyed God, and traveled to the stream, hiding from King Ahab. He was lonely, but he was safe there for a while. He had the stream to drink from, and the ravens brought him food twice a day. But then the stream dried up. There was a drought in the land.

God told Elijah it was time to move on. He could stay by the stream no longer. God directed Elijah to travel to the home of a widow who lived in Zarephath. This widow would provide food, shelter, and drink for Elijah.

Elijah and the Widow

When Elijah reached Zarephath, he found the widow collecting sticks for her fire. Elijah asked her for some water and bread. There was very little water because of the drought, but the widow generously shared what she was able to spare. The widow did not have any bread, just some flour. There was not much left. After she made one more loaf, she would be out of flour.

Elijah told the woman to make him some bread, and then make some for herself. The widow was confused, she had already explained to the man that she did not have enough flour for two loaves. Elijah replied,

"The bowl of flour shall not be exhausted, nor shall the jar of oil be empty, until the day that the Lord sends rain on the face of the earth."

1 Kings 17:14

The widow trusted that Elijah was speaking what he had been told by God, and made two loaves of bread. Not only was there enough, but there was also more! They were able to eat well for many days. As God predicted, the widow invited the prophet to stay with her.

Elijah stayed with the widow for three years. He even saved the life of her son. One day, when her son was very sick, she could not hear him breathe. Elijah took the boy in his arms, and began to pray, as he breathed on him. After the third time, the boy took a deep breath and sat up. He was cured! The widow was very grateful. She was thankful that she had trusted Elijah and provided for him. Her kindness to a stranger allowed her son to live.

Elijah and King Ahab Meets Again

Drought and famine were causing all the people in the land to suffer. God told Elijah to go speak with King Ahab again. Elijah was afraid to be near the evil man, but God promised that if Elijah obeyed, He would make it rain. The drought and famine would finally come to an end!

Elijah met King Ahab while the king was out looking for water. The king was filled with rage with he saw Elijah. The wicked king blamed Elijah for the drought and famine. Elijah defended himself, telling the king that it was not his fault. He was simply the messenger of God. It was the fault of the king, his family, and their evil behavior. The land was suffering because their ruler had turned his back on God. When they changed how they acted, the drought would be lifted, and the famine would end.

Elijah challenged King Ahab, telling him to bring all the prophets to the false god Baal to the top of Mount Carmel. The prophets of Baal would sacrifice to their god, and Elijah would sacrifice to his God. They would whether Baal or God would answer their prayers.

The king could not resist a challenge, so he did as Elijah asked. A large group of people came to watch. They were followers of Baal. When everyone reached the top of the mountain, Elijah asked the people when they would accept the true God, and turn away from Baal. They did not answer.

The four hundred and fifty prophets of Baal made fires and prepared to make sacrifices. They got ready to call their God and god. The prophets of Baal made a sacrifice that morning and afternoon. There was no response. Elijah did not make a morning or afternoon sacrifice.

There was a damaged altar to God on the mountain. When it was almost time for the evening sacrifice, Elijah called the followers of Baal over to the altar. As they watched, he repaired the broken altar. He surrounded the altar with twelve stones. One stone for each tribe of Israel. He dug a trench around the altar. The sacrifice to God was placed on the altar.

Elijah asked the followers of Baal to help him prepare for the sacrifice. Following his directions, they filled four buckets with water and poured it over the wood for the fire. They did this three times until the water flowed off the altar and filled the trench.

It was finally time for the evening sacrifice. Elijah prayed to God. He told God that he had done everything He had asked him to do. Elijah asked God to answer him, to show Baal's followers that He was the one true God.

Suddenly, a great fire broke out on the wet wood.

The sacrifice burned, and all the water was dried up by the heat. When Baal's followers saw this, they fell to the ground. They now knew that there was one true God.

Baal's prophets began to flee down the mountain. Elijah yelled at the people to not let them escape. They could not be allowed to continue to infect the nation and its people with their false beliefs and wicked ways. After that night, there were no more prophets of Baal. The false god was destined to be forgotten.

That evening, the rains returned, and the people were grateful. The drought was over!

Chapter 30: Naaman Is Healed

(2 Kings 5)

Naaman was a captain of the army. He served the king of Aram. He was well known and very respected. He brought victory to the people of God. Unfortunately, Naaman had a horrible skin disease called leprosy. In this time, there was no cure for the disease, and it was very contagious. People who had leprosy were usually made to leave their homes, and live alone in the wilderness, or with other people who had the same disease.

While fighting in the army, Naaman had brought back a young girl from Israel to be a servant for his wife. They treated her well, and she was happy living with them. The little girl hoped to be able to help Naaman. She told Naaman's wife about a prophet she'd heard of back home in Israel. She thought that the prophet could heal Naaman!

Naaman told the King of Aram what the little girl had said. The king encouraged Naaman to go find a cure. The king of Aram promised to send a letter to the king of Israel, asking him to help Naaman find this prophet. Along with the letter, the king of Aram sent silver, gold, and beautiful clothes as gifts.

The king of Israel was very upset when he read the letter. Leprosy could not be cured! The king of Israel was afraid that the king of Aram was asking him to do something impossible. He feared that the king of Aram would use his failure to help as an excuse to start a war.

When he heard about his king's reaction, Elisha, the prophet, tried to calm him down. Elisha asked permission to see Naaman when he arrived in Israel. He believed that he could cure him. The king of Israel agreed. They could at least try to prevent a war.

When Naaman arrived in Israel, he found his way to Elijah's home. Instead of meeting him at the door, Elisha sent a messenger to speak with Naaman. The messenger said to Naaman, "Go to the River Jordan and wash your body seven times. This will cure your leprosy."

Naaman stormed away. He was very angry! He had come all this way just to be told to clean him. He was not an unclean person. He had washed more than seven times since he had gotten the disease. Why would the water here be any different from the water in his own country?

Naaman's servants tried to make him feel better. The pointed out that Naaman would not have complained if the prophet had given him a difficult task. He would have taken on the task with no questions or arguments. They suggested that he at least try. He'd already come all this way!

Naaman agreed to at least try. He had been expecting a dramatic ceremony with prayer and sacrifice, but a good wash never hurt anyone. As Naaman stepped out of the River Jordan for the seventh time, his skin was clear, and he was cured!

Chapter 31: King Hezekiah

(2 Kings 18-19)

King Hezekiah became the ruler of Israel and the age of twenty-nine. His father, King David, was a wicked man who worshipped false gods. King Hezekiah was very different from his father. He was a good man who was dedicated to God. King Hezekiah prayed often and tore down altars and temples his father had built for false gods. King Hezekiah hired workers to repair the damage done to God's temples during his father's time as ruler.

God blessed King Hezekiah for his devotion. God led the king to victory during many battles against the godless Philistines.

After King Hezekiah had been ruling for fourteen years, King Sennacherib of Assyria captured many cities of Judah. King Hezekiah sent a message to King Sennacherib, asking what he could do to protect his lands. King Sennacherib asked for a huge amount of gold and silver.

King Hezekiah thought that he had no choice. He must protect his people. King Hezekiah decided to give King Sennacherib everything that he had asked for. King Hezekiah gave King Sennacherib all the gold and silver that was in his own treasury, and the treasury's of God's temples.

King Hezekiah even had to take gold and silver out of temples dedicated to God. He ripped down the doors made of gold. King Hezekiah hated to do this, but he hoped God would understand. After all, he was trying to free God's people!

King Sennacherib was happy to accept all the gold and silver King Hezekiah sent him. However, the evil king sent his armies anyway! The general of King Sennacherib's army shouted threats to King Hezekiah's people. King Sennacherib told the people their king could not save them; their only chance was to abandon King Hezekiah and God. King Sennacherib made fun to the people for trusting in God. The people were very scared, but they followed King Hezekiah's directions and did not respond.

King Hezekiah went to his temple to pray to God to guide him. He sent three messengers to visit the prophet, Isaiah. The prophet told the messengers to report back to King Hezekiah. They were to pass along the message to keep hope. Stay faithful to God. King Sennacherib would be sent back to his own lands and would be punished.

King Sennacherib sent a letter to King Hezekiah. The letter said that King Hezekiah could not defend his city. God would not be able to save him. King Hezekiah took this letter to the temple and prayed to God.

God sent his answer through the prophet Isaiah. He had heard King Hezekiah's prayer, and would protect the city! King Sennacherib would not harm His people.

"He will not come to this city or shoot an arrow there, and he will not come before it with a shield or throw up a siege ramp against it. By the way that he came, by the same he will return, and he shall not come to this city... For I will defend this city to save it for My own sake and for My servant David's sake."

2 Kings 19:32-34

That night, God moved through the King Sennacherib's camp. That morning, none of the soldiers woke up. The king was alone. He could not take over King Hezekiah's city by himself.

Kin Sennacherib went home in defeat. King Hezekiah and his people celebrated their victory. Thanks to God, they were all safe, and had not even had to fight! They continued to worship God and walk His path.

Chapter 32: Jonah

(Jonah 1-4)

God asked Jonah to travel to Nineveh. The people of Nineveh had turned against God and were behaving in wicked ways. Jonah believed in God but chose to disobey Him. Jonah did not want to travel to Nineveh. Instead, Jonah got on a boat that was traveling to Tarshish.

God was angry that Jonah had not obeyed him. To show his anger, he called up a violent storm. The wind was so fast and the waves were so rough that the boat was about to break! The rain was coming down so hard that they could not see where they were going.

The sailors were not men of God. They prayed to false gods to save them. No help came. They threw whatever they could spare off the side of the boat, in hopes that a lighter load would keep the storm from sinking them.

Somehow, Jonah managed to sleep through the start of the storm. The captain of the ship had to come to wake him up. Since the gods of the sailors were not helping, the captain hoped that Jonah's God would bring them to safety. The captain asked Jonah to pray to God. Jonah confessed to the captain and sailors that he was on the boat against God's wishes. He believed that the storm was God's way of punishing him for his disobedience.

Jonah knew he should have listened to God. Because he had disobeyed, everyone on the ship was in danger. The storm grew worse. Jonah asked the men to throw him off the boat. He was willing to sacrifice himself to save the others.

At first, the sailors refused. They tried to steer the ship to land. They even gave up their gods and began praying for God to save them. The storm continued to blow. Finally, the sailors had no choice. To save their lives, they did as Jonah had asked, and threw him into the sea.

When Jonah hit the water, a whale swallowed him whole! The seas calmed, the winds slowed to a gentle breeze, and the sun began to shine once more. The sailors prayed their thanks to God. They vowed to follow in His path and made offerings and sacrifices to him.

While Jonah was inside the whale, he had plenty of time to think. He was ashamed that he had disobeyed God and put other people in danger. He prayed to God, asking for forgiveness. After three days, the whale swam close to shore, and spit Jonah out! Jonah swam to shore unharmed.

God repeated his earlier instructions to Jonah. He should go to Nineveh and spread God's word. Jonah had learned his lesson! He packed up his things and headed to Nineveh.

When Jonah reached Nineveh, he told the people that unless they started to worship and obey God, their city would be ruined in forty days.

The people of Nineveh listened to Jonah! They began to pray to God, and follow His commandments. They were sorry for the wicked things they had done. Even the king started to have faith. When God saw that the people where changing, He changed his mind, and decided not to destroy the city.

Even though the people were listening to Jonah, he was still unhappy. He did not like living in Nineveh. He did not care that God was going to save the city, he just wanted to leave.

Jonah decided to leave the city. He was afraid to go far, so he built himself a small shelter right outside of the city walls. It was very hot in the desert, so God gave Jonah a plant for shade. Jonah was very proud of this plant. That night, worms started to eat the plant, and it died. Jonah was very uncomfortable in his shelter. The sun was too hot. Even the breeze was hot. Jonah was very angry that his plant had died.

God spoke to Jonah and told him that it was wrong to be angry the plant had died. Jonah had done nothing to help the plant grow, he had just accepted the gift. Jonah was angry for the loss of his plant, that he had only had one day, but he did not care that God had saved an entire city.

By telling them how to follow God, hundreds of thousands of people and animals had been saved in Nineveh. Despite this, Jonah cared only about losing the plant that gave him comfort. By giving him a plant, then taking it away, God taught Jonah that it was important to care about others. All people have value, not just the people that you like.

"You had compassion on the plant for which you did not work and which you did not cause to grow, which came overnight and perished overnight. Should I not have compassion on Nineveh, the great city in which there are more than 120,000 persons who do not know the difference between their right and left hand, as well as many animals?

Jonah 4:9-11

Chapter 33: The Lions' Den

(Daniel 6)

K ing Darius picked Daniel as a leader in the kingdom. He was a very wise man. Other men were very jealous of Daniel's wisdom and his high rank, so they hated him. He was given a lot of responsibility throughout the kingdom.

Through no fault of his own, Daniel developed many enemies. They plotted against Daniel and tried to get him in trouble with King Darius. The examined his work closely, trying to find proof that he had done something wrong. They could not find the smallest bit of proof. Daniel loyal to his king.

Daniel was well known as a faithful man of God. Daniel's enemies decided to use this against him. They tricked King Darius into agreeing to a new law. This law said that for thirty days, his people could only ask King Darius for advice or permission. Anyone who asked for help from someone else who be thrown into a den. Not just any den, but a den where lions lived!

Daniel knew about the law, but he continued to be faithful to God. Daniel prayed to God three times a day. Daniel's enemies reported him to the king. King Darius was very upset. He liked and respected Daniel! King Darius was not trying to keep people from praying! But, he had signed the law and had to follow it.

Reluctantly, King Darius gave the command to throw Daniel into the lions' den. The king tried to comfort Daniel, telling him that God would protect him. Once Daniel was thrown into the den, it was sealed with a large stone, and the king's ring.

King Darius miserably returned to the palace. He refused to eat or drink. He refused any entertainment. He did not want to hear music plays, songs being sung, or see any dancing. He was so worried that he was unable to sleep.

The next morning, King Darius left the palace very early. He rushed to the lions' den but had little hope that Daniel would be alive. When the king reached the den, he called out to Daniel. King Darius was very happy to hear a response other than the roar of a lion!

"O king, live forever! My God sent His angel and shut the lions' mouths and they have not harmed me... O king, I have committed no crime."
Daniel 6:21-22

King Darius happily ordered his men to free Daniel from the lions' den. Because of his faith in God, Daniel did not have one scratch or bite mark.

King Darius now realized that Daniel's enemies had tricked him. They got him to sign the law, knowing that Daniel would continue to pray to God. King Darius ordered his evil men to the punishment they had planned for Daniel. The men were thrown into the lions' den! Just to be safe, King Darius ordered that their families be thrown into the lions' den as well. They were not people of God, so the lions ate them before they even reached the bottom.

King Darius announced to his people that they should all obey God, and have faith in the God of Daniel.

"For He is the living God and enduring forever,
And his kingdom is one which will not be
destroyed,
And His dominion will be forever.
He delivers and rescues and performs signs and
wonders
In heaven and on earth,
Who has also delivered Daniel from the power of
the lions."

Daniel 6:26-27

Daniel continued to serve King Darius faithfully. He never doubted his faith in God. There was peace during the king's rule.

Chapter 34: The New King

(Isaiah 9-11)

As the years went on, more wicked people became powerful. They captured God's people and forced them to work as slaves. Living with the captives was a prophet named Ezekiel. God spoke to Ezekiel, giving him hope. Ezekiel spread the word to his people, God would send a new king to save and lead them. This new king would bring peace to God's people.

People that had strayed from God would be guided back to His path. Their nation will expand, as they are freed from slavery. God's people would have to fight, but a child would be born who would lead them. Suffering will come to an end. The light will shine through the nations once again.

God's nations will grow, and His people will be happy. Joy will fill their hearts, and rich harvests will fill their fields. There will be no droughts, nor floods. God will take away the troubles of His people. Their enemies will no longer be able to harm them.

When a child of God is born, wars will end. People will no longer spend their days on the battlefield. This son of God will lead the people. He will be called the "Prince of Peace." He will rule for all time.

"For a child will be born to us, a son will be given to us;
And the government will rest on His shoulders;
And His name will be called Wonderful Counselor, Mighty God,
Eternal Father, Prince of Peace."
Isaiah 9:6

God will punish the people that have oppressed His followers. The altars and temples to false gods will be destroyed. God's people will rebuild to honor Him. God will not take pity of the enemies of His people. Fire will spread, burning away wickedness. The fields that were destroyed will now provide even better harvests. The trees that were cut down will be replaced by newly planted ones. They will grow even taller, stronger, and provide more shade.

"His anger does not turn away
And his Hand is still stretched out."
Isaiah 9:21

God will punish all those who act against him. Those who build statues of false gods. Those who make unfair laws. Those who are not kind and generous to the poor. Those that are unkind to

orphans. People who turn against each other.
To avoid punishment, lawmakers must be fair. People must help those that are less fortunate than themselves.

Those who do not obey God will be put into prison. People who say they trust in God but do not act according to God's law will be punished.

A man will be born, descended from Jesse, who will speak God's word. He will be fair. He will punish the evil people, and reward the good. He will unite and save the people of God.

This new king will not judge people by the way they look. He will judge them fairly, by their words and actions.

Animals will live in peace. They will not fight. Small children will be safe around the largest lion and snakes with the sharpest fangs. They will not bite or strike.

People will no longer hurt each other. They will

not want to destroy things. They will find that knowledge and kindness are more important than pride and power.

The countries throughout the world that were at war will now be at peace. People will no longer be jealous of each other. Kindness, joy, and peace will spread throughout the nations of the world. The people of God will be happy. The people of God will be saved.

"And he will lift up a standard for the nations
And assemble the banished ones of Israel,
And will gather the dispersed of Judah
From the four corners of the earth."
Isaiah 11:12

Conclusion

Dear Listener,

T hank you for listening to the *Bible Story Book For Kids:* True Bible Stories For Children About God And The Old Testament Every Christian Child Should Know! I hope you enjoyed listening the stories and learned something as well. As you can see, the Bible can be just as exciting as the other books you read or listened to and movies you watched.

Some of these stories may be frightening. God in the Old Testament can be frightening and mean. It is important to remember that He just wanted His people to obey Him and walk with Him. The people that God punished turned against Him and were wicked. They didn't just do the occasional bad thing, they became bad people.

God made many promises throughout the Bible on not repeating His punishments. We've never seen a flood like Noah did, or rains of fire! God no longer comes to earth to punish people. He watches over us, taking care of us from above.

Walk with God, and He will bless you. He is always with you. God is forgiving. All you need to do is ask Him.

"THE WORD IS NEAR YOU, IN YOUR MOUTH AND IN YOUR HEART"—that is, the word of faith that we are preaching is that if you confess with your mouth Jesus as Lord and believe in your heart that God raised Him from the dead, you will be saved—for with the heart a person believes, resulting in righteousness; and with the mouth he confesses, resulting in salvation.

(Romans 10:8-10)

If you have any questions about what you have read, ask your parents or guardian. They will be happy to talk about it with you!

Praise God and his son, Christ Jesus, Lord of Lords and King of Kings.

Amen!

Book 2:
Bible Story Book for Kids:
The New Testament

True Bible Stories For Children About Jesus And The New Testament Every Christian Child Should Know

Introduction

C ongratulations on downloading the Bible Story Book For Kids: True Bible Stories For Children About Jesus And The New Testament Every Christian Child Should Know! This Beginner's Bible is presented to educate young girls and boys about the life and ministry of the Lord Jesus Christ. It covers his Birth, Ministry, Death, Resurrection, and Ascension—as well as the resulting Christian Church that followed him. It is the Greatest Story Ever Told—about how it was possible for one man to have mankind's sins be salvaged and bring everyone to a life of following and upholding God's will.

Parents—in a world so busy, so beautiful, so interesting, and often so confusing—some of us think that we don't have time for God. However, for those who are aware of him, we can understand the peace that a prayerful life can bring to a soul. Even the little children have daily challenges and daily choices—and imparting a love of God into their heart at an early age is a wonderful gift for a fabulous life. To a child, prayer is a natural instinct. As we raise our children to do good, to live with the principles you are teaching them, it is also important to teach them the power and importance of prayer. In this world, you represent God to a young child—giving them their needs often before they even ask. God encourages all of us to teach them that it is ultimately God who supplies all of our needs.

Jesus Christ had a special fondness for children because of their innocence and willingness to accept His words without objection. God promised in the Old Testament that if parents would raise up their children in the belief of God and His Holy word, they would have a firm foundation for their entire life—and God sees us all, no matter the age, as His children. He loves all of us and only wants the best for each and every one of us.

The stories about Jesus Christ and what he did are presented in a brief, simple format, suitable to be studied with your children or read to them at night as they drift off to sleep. Simple words have been used as much as possible—with explanations for more difficult things so that the children can understand.

Lifted from the New American Standard Bible (NASB) are the italicized scriptures in this book. Some of the scriptures included in the stories have been paraphrased so that they could be clearly understood and taught.

The Bible is one of the most amazing miracles God ever performed and is written so that the youngest child to someone who studied it for his whole life can constantly find deeper and deeper levels of understanding about the God's unending compassion for all of mankind. It is our hope and prayer for this book to start a journey that will last an entire lifetime of learning about God and loving him as a personal Father, to experience a rebirth as God's creation, then eventually being with God and Jesus Christ through all eternity to come.

There exists a plethora of literature on this topic on the internet—I genuinely appreciate your decision to pick this one! Rest assured that all possible work was done to guarantee that this book is as jam-packed and abundant in details as it possibly can. Enjoy!

1. A Visit by an Angel

*And behold, you will conceive in your womb
and bear a son, and you shall name Him Jesus.
He will be great and will be called the Son of the
Most High; and the Lord God will give Him the
throne of His father David, and He will reign
over the house of Jacob forever, and His
kingdom will have no end."*
(Luke 1:31-33)

A long, long time ago, in a tiny county called Israel, there was a beautiful young lady whose name was Mary. She lived in a little farming village called Nazareth. All the lands around Lake Kinnereth had roll hills, little fishing villages, farms, and a few bigger towns that were collectively called the Land of Galilee. The people were peaceful, worked hard, loved God, and went to their church called a synagogue to worship God and hear the readings of the ancient scrolls that held the words of all the prophets.

In the ancient writings of the prophets (what we now call the Old Testament), mankind was said to be earthed by the Father Almighty—but the foremost of his kind, Adam, sinned against God, which gave rule over the earth to a fallen angel. The angel was originally called Lucifer, but he came to be called the Devil—or Satan. For thousands of years, Satan brought death and destruction to everyone, and the people cried over and over for a Savior to save the world from its sins to ultimately have them come back to the Father. Ancient prophets all talked about this man who would one day come, and the people waited through the years for him to be born.

God had chosen a man named Abram as His creation's father and given a promised land to his children forever. The children of Abraham grew and went through many adventures and mishaps, which became recorded in what we call today the *Old Testament* and what the Jews call the *Torah*. It was recorded that God promised to Eve that a child would be born one day that would rule the world. Throughout time, all the prophets saw his coming and swore for a king who'd save mankind. Mary was smart and kind and raised by her parents to love God and to know His magnificent works and creations for her kind, the Judeans, written about in the ancient scrolls in their church called a synagogue; like Joseph saving the Israelites from the famine; or like Moses parting the Red Sea the morning after the first Passover. Her hometown was mostly a quiet farming town—full of people who worked hard, went to their church every weekend, and raised their families according to the laws of God.

However, in those days, Nazareth and all of Israel was ruled over by a mean, far-away kingdom called Rome. Even though Rome was far away, they had a governor that controlled the country and had many soldiers that bossed around the people and made them pay taxes to the mean Roman emperor whose name was Caesar Augustus—and a king he appointed over Israel, an even meaner man named King Herod. Nobody in Nazareth liked either one of them and hated having to pay taxes so that King Herod could build things for Emperor Augustus and for himself.

One big city in Galilee, next to the lake, was called Caesarea Philippi, having been built by the Romans with the Jewish tax money to honor the Roman emperor. Another big city, west of Galilee, called Caesarea, was a port being built by King Herod on the Mediterranean coast, with statues of Emperor Augustus and King Herod all around the city—and the people there worshipped all kinds of other gods.

This Mary loved a young man in the village called Joseph. Joseph was a carpenter—he built things out of wood like tables and chairs and many other things. He was respected in his village because he always concentrated on his work and built the best things for the people to use in their houses. Joseph loved Mary very much as well—and so, one day, he went to Mary's parents and asked if they would let him Mary marry him. They were happy and said yes because they knew that Joseph was a fine young man, successful in his business, and would be able to take good care of their daughter and bring them beautiful grandchildren as well.

Mary was very happy to find out that her parents said she could marry Joseph, and both began to prepare for the wedding. Joseph had to fix up his house so that he could have room when Mary moved in, and Mary had to prepare her wedding dress and buy special jewelry to wear in her hair on her wedding day.

One night, when Mary was laying in her bed thinking about her upcoming wedding and how wonderful it would be to be married to Joseph, she was surprised when a man appeared out of nothing in her bedroom. "Don't be scared Mary—I am not here to hurt you. I am an angel, and my name is Gabriel. God sent me, and I have come to tell you something very important."

Mary knew about angels from the ancient texts they read in church and immediately calmed down. "Yes, angel Gabriel, I understand. What have you come to tell me?"

The angel said, "I am to tell you that you are going to be pregnant and have a baby—and he is a very special child. He will become the King of Israel, like your ancestor King David, and he will rule the land forever."

Now, Mary had a puzzled look on her face and thought about places in the ancient scrolls that promised a king would be born someday that would rule over Israel like a lion and would be loving and wonderful and not at all like the

Romans who were always mean to them and took pride in bossing them around.

However, Mary was puzzled by the fact that she was engaged to Joseph but not married yet, so she asked the angel how it was possible that she could become pregnant and have a baby.

Gabriel told her not to worry—that God was going to make her pregnant and that nothing was impossible for God. God wanted a son that He could call his own. He also told Mary that her cousin, Elizabeth, who lived in another town, was pregnant, too, even though she was too old to have a baby.

Mary accepted what the angel said and replied to Gabriel, "Behold the handmaid of the Lord. Be it unto me according to your word." At that very instant, Mary became pregnant with God's baby, and the angel Gabriel disappeared.

Mary soon went to Elizabeth's village and found out that yes, as the angel had told her, Elizabeth was very pregnant. When they saw each other and hugged hello, both babies in their bellies kicked their mommies, leaping for joy! Mary remained in her friend's home within the next 3 months, helping Elizabeth around the house so that she could be comfortable and have a happy baby.

Elizabeth told Mary all about what had happened to her. She had been very sad because she thought she was cursed, having been married for many years but never had been able to have a baby. The same angel Gabriel came to her husband, Zacharias, who was one of the priests in the Temple. Gabriel came while he was in the Temple and promised that she would become pregnant and that they would have a son. The angel said that he would become the messenger to pave the way for the new king who was coming after him, and he was to name the baby John. However, Zacharias didn't believe what the angel had said, and he was made speechless.

While she was there helping Elizabeth, Mary's own belly began to grow bigger and bigger, too. After the three months, Mary eventually had to go home—but when she came to say hi to her boyfriend, Joseph, he realized that she was pregnant, and he knew it wasn't his because they weren't married yet. He was very upset with Mary and thought for days and days what he should do about it. He loved Mary very much, but he thought he should call off the wedding because she was pregnant with someone else's baby. He thought maybe he should break off the engagement.

Then one night, Joseph was sleeping and tossing and turning in his bed, and he had a dream. The same angel, Gabriel, came to him in the dream and assured him that the baby was God's baby and that he needed to go ahead and marry Mary as soon as possible.

And so, as soon as the arrangements could be finished, Joseph and Mary had a big celebration before the whole town of Nazareth, and they were married. They were very happy and kept the secret from everyone that she was pregnant on her wedding day.

Now, several months later, Elizabeth was finally ready to have her baby. After 8 days, they had him christened at the Temple. When he was asked what the child's name would be, he wrote on a tablet that he would be called John, as he still couldn't speak. Immediately, he was able to talk and praise God.

2. Jesus Is Born

She gave birth to her firstborn, a son. She wrapped him in cloths and placed him in a manger because there was no guest room available for them. . . . But the angel said to them, "Do not be afraid—for behold, I bring you good news of great joy, which will be for all the people—for today, in the city of David, there has been born for you a Savior, who is Christ the Lord.

(Luke 2:7. 10-11)

After Joseph and Mary were married, a Roman soldier came to Nazareth and told everyone in the village that they have to travel at a certain time to the town their ancestors came from to be counted for a census. A census is a list of names, where they lived, and what they did for a living. Emperor Augustus had wanted to know all the names of the people he rules in Israel. Both Joseph and Mary were descended from King David, whose hometown was a little village near Jerusalem called Bethlehem, so that was where they knew they had to go.

Mary was very pregnant, close to having the baby—but they had to go, or they would get into a lot of trouble. Hence, they packed up a horse, with a cart behind it, and Joseph drove the horse while pulling Mary in the cart behind him. A bunch of other families from Nazareth went with them. People didn't usually travel alone in those days because of dangers that could happen on a trip. When they got close to Bethlehem, some of the other families went off to the towns and villages they had to go to, but some of them stayed with Joseph and Mary all the way to Bethlehem.

When they got there, Joseph found a shady spot for Mary to wait, and he went to all the places in town that had rooms for visitors—but everyone was already full of people coming to Bethlehem for the census. He looked and looked all day, but he couldn't find a single empty room. He told everyone that his wife was very pregnant, but they couldn't help him at all.

Finally, at the last place he tried, Joseph told the man running the Inn that he desperately needed a room because his wife was very pregnant and about to have her baby. The man told him that his Inn was already full, but they could sleep in a stable he owned for his horses and donkeys and sheep. Joseph gladly accepted the offer so that he could get Mary into any place rather than laying in the cart.

The stable had a large open area in the middle, which is called a manger—full of hay and water and tools for feeding the animals, with stalls all around that caged the animals in. The stable smelled sweet with the hay, and the man who owned it had kept it clean. Joseph helped Mary out of the cart and into the manger and made a bed for her to lay in out of the hay so that he could rest after the long trip there. The nice man who owned the house and the stable brought them food and water while they were his guests.

The lines to sign the census list was very long, and they had to wait a few days until they could sign it. While they were waiting, one evening, Mary began to feel her baby moving, and Mary started to have the baby. Soon, the little baby boy was born, and Joseph took the baby and cleaned it off.

Then, Joseph took the baby and wrapped a cloth around it that had been soaked in water and salt, to show God that he was committing the baby to Him and that he would do his best to raise up the baby to be kind and honest and have a love for God always. The cloth, which was called swaddling clothes, was only wrapped around the baby for a few moments while the parents would pray for the baby to be safe and healthy and happy. It was a tradition that the Jews of the time did for all newborn babies. He remembered what the angel Gabriel had told both—that God had said to call him Jesus, so Joseph did just that and laid the baby down into Mary's arms.

During the moments when the Son of God was being delivered, an angel by the name of Gabriel appeared in the hills that surround Bethlehem. There was a group of young men sitting around a campfire, watching over their herds of sheep sleeping in the fields. The land was still full of wolves and other animals that loved to eat sheep, so they had to be guarded day and night by shepherds. These young men were all devoted to God and went to church every week to worship him.

The angel appeared to the shepherds, with a radiant glow all around him, and the shepherds became scared at the sight because they had never seen an angel before. "Do not worry," Gabriel said, "because I have come to tell you some great news."

"Tonight, a baby was born in Bethlehem who is the Messiah God promised would come to Israel, who will become the King of Kings. You go to the Inn in Bethlehem, and you will find the baby still wrapped up in the swaddling clothes, lying in the manger with his mother, Mary."

Just then, all around them, many other angels appeared, praising God about the baby. They all said together, "Glory to God in the highest, and on earth peace—Goodwill toward men."

After all the angels disappeared, the shepherds immediately ran into Bethlehem and found the Inn and went into the stable—and just like the angel Gabriel had told them, they arrived just when Joseph was putting the baby into Mary's arms, still wrapped in its swaddling clothes. They were so excited, that they hugged Joseph and kissed Mary and the baby on their cheeks—then, they praised God that the new king had been born. They ran to tell all their friends that they had been visited by angels and seen the newborn baby who would be the King. All the people who heard the story were amazed and hopeful that the king that they had hoped for was born.

The next week, they had their baby christened in one of the temples of Jerusalem. They bought two young pigeons outside to be sacrificed in the Temple. When they were there, they encountered two very old people who had prayed for all their lives that they wouldn't die before seeing the promised King from God. Their names were Simon and Anna, and both of them were given the Holy Spirit and prophesied wonderful things when they saw the baby. Simon took the baby and prayed to God in front of Joseph and Mary, saying: "Now, Lord, You are releasing Your bond-servant to depart in peace, according to Your word; for my eyes have seen Your salvation, which You have prepared in the presence of all peoples, A LIGHT OF REVELATION TO THE GENTILES, and the glory of Your people in Israel."

Anna, an 84-year old woman, was also there to watch and praise the newborn. Joseph and Mary's eyes opened wide to see and hear these things said about their baby.

3. The Bright Star and The Three Visitors

Now, after Jesus was born in Bethlehem of Judea, in the days of Herod the king, magi from the east arrived in Jerusalem and said, "Where is He who has been born King of the Jews? For we saw His star in the east and have come to worship Him."
(Matthew 2:1-2)

After the baby was born, Joseph was able to sign the census and take Mary and the baby back to Nazareth. At the same time, far away, a group of men who studied the stars had been watching wonderful things happening. Stars were lining up in ways they had never seen before—the king planet Jupiter lining up with the constellation Regulus and the constellation Leo, the lion. They wondered what it all meant.

Hundreds of years before, the astronomers of a country called Persia had been taught by a very wise man named Daniel, that someday there would be born in Israel a king whose kingdom would never end. God revealed His entire plan for mankind in the stars, in their formations called constellations, and the movements of the heavenly bodies. The astronomers who watched for these signs were called Magi because they had special secrets like magicians. They all knew and trusted that Daniel received these things from God, because God had shown Daniel secrets in the king's dreams, and protected him when he was cast into a lion's den. Every generation of Magi taught the young astronomers all about the prophecies of Daniel and watched the skies every night for the heavenly ciphers of the King's arrival.

Now, finally, it was here! Sign after the sign

appeared in the stars, and they were convinced that the king had been born. "We must go worship him," they said to themselves. They packed up their camels full of all sorts of precious items to give to the newborn king. They were gold and rare spices called frankincense and myrrh.

After many days, the Magi finally had prepared for the long trip from Persia to the capital of Israel, Jerusalem. They went to the king of Israel, a very mean man named King Herod, and asked to see the newborn king. Herod was very mad and said I don't know anything about a newborn king. I am the King of Israel. Where did you hear that some other king was born?"

The magi told old King Herod about all the signs in the skies, and the prophecies about the king who would be born and rule forever. They told him about a prophecy in the ancient scrolls that the baby came from Bethlehem, David's city and that it happened about two months before.

Since they didn't get any help from mean old King Herod, they got back on their camels and traveled the short distance to from Jerusalem to Bethlehem and asked about the newborn king. Many of the townspeople knew of it, from the wondrous stories told to them by the shepherds about that night. The townspeople told the Magi that the parents were only visiting Bethlehem for the census and that they had returned to their own village of Nazareth.

Knowing now where to go, the Magi took their camels again and traveled north to the Sea of Galilee, and found the town of Nazareth, and the house of Joseph the Carpenter there. Joseph let them in, and there they found the young child playing on the floor with his mother. Baby Jesus was now almost two months old.

The Magi told Joseph and Mary that they had come from very far away, to honor the newborn king and to bring him presents. They unpacked the camels and brought in jars full of gold coins, and spices, and rich cloth for the baby. Mary was simply amazed how many times and ways God had shown her and Joseph that this little boy was the future king that all the prophets had promised in the past!

But after the Magi left, the angel Gabriel warned him to take the baby to Egypt, as King Herod was searching for the young child that would become a future king. King Herod had demanded the death of every child below the age of 2 living in Bethlehem. The Magi had told King Herod approximately how old the boy was at that time. Hundreds of young babies were taken from their parents and killed. But since the boy he was searching for had returned to Nazareth, the angel warned Joseph that King Herod would be looking for them there next! So, Joseph took Mary and the young child, and immediately packed up their things and traveled down into Egypt. It was just a little while until King Herod died, and they were able to return to Nazareth without fearing for the life of Jesus.

4. Jesus Is Lost

Then, after three days, they found Him in the temple, sitting in the midst of the teachers, both listening to them and asking them questions.
(Luke 2:46)

N
ow, Joseph and Mary took great care raising the child Jesus. Because Joseph was a successful carpenter, he made a good income to raise his family, and they were able to use the gold and rare spices when they had to buy things—and Mary had other babies, boys, and girls—among them were James, Joseph, Jude, Simon, and their sisters, too.

Jesus was just like other regular children growing up. He had toys and friends to play with. He had to learn to read and go to school and to church to become a smart child.

Joseph and Mary followed all the laws of Moses and raised their family well, taking them to the synagogue every weekend—and on three special holy days, they all traveled together to the big city, Jerusalem. The Jews had special holidays called Passover in the spring, Pentecost in the summer, and Tabernacles in the fall. All Judeans were supposed to at least come to Jerusalem on those holidays and worship at the Temple, a sort of big church, to honor God by following the laws of Moses. Joseph and Mary went every year according to the law of Moses.

In that time, it was dangerous to travel alone, so families would get together into a large group, called a caravan, and the men would ride together with the other men, the women together with the women, and the children together with all the other children. Of course, the children traveled with one or more babysitters who would make sure they were taken care of. At night, the families would all be reunited to share their meals and night time together.

During the Passover in Jesus' 12th year, they visited Jerusalem. The beautiful Temple in Jerusalem, built by King Herod on the site of the earlier Temple built by King Solomon, was a wonder to behold, and filled with people from all over. It was built out of white limestone blocks, with an outer courtyard for anyone to come into, and an inner courtyard that only Jews could go into, and a special room that is solely accessible to the High Priest. There, the High Priest sacrificed annually in the Holy of Hollies for the sins of all Jewish people to be forgiven.

At the feast of Passover, extended families got together for wonderful meals, lambs and unleavened bread and tart greens to remind them all the miracle of God saving the people by Moses, when the angel of Death killed all the first-born Egyptian children and passed over Israelite children. It also remembered Red Sea's miracles by parting as they left Egypt and went to Mount Sinai. They went to the Temple and heard the blessings of the priests, and saw the High Priest go into the Holy of Holiness to ask that God forgave all the sins of the Jews from the previous year.

When the feast days were over, Joseph and the men of his village gathered everyone together for the long trip back home. Once again, the men traveled together, the women together, and all the children in the rear. They traveled all day long and had gotten part way home when they stopped to camp for the evening.

Mary went to where all the children were gathered, and found her sons, James, Joseph, Jude and Simon, and their sisters, but where was Jesus? Nobody had seen him, and the babysitters had not realized that he was gone.

"Oh no," Mary cried, "We have lost our precious son, the promised King." She started to cry and shake, remembering all the things that the angel had said about him, but Joseph calmed her down. "We will go back together to find him," he told her.

The next morning, they left the camp early, after asking a friend to take care of the rest of their family while they searched for their older brother. As quickly as they could, Joseph and Mary returned to Jerusalem, reaching it at nightfall. There was no way to search the crowded city at night, so they found a room and nervously slept together.

The next morning, they went searching for Jesus. They went from house to house, asking where there lost son might be. Finally, one of the men in the city said, "I think I saw a young boy who sounds like him at the Temple yesterday." Joseph and Mary ran to the Temple as fast as they could, through narrow alleys clogged with people. When they finally got there, they asked the Temple guards if they had seen the boy. They said, "yes," there is a boy about that age meeting with the high priests right now."

Joseph and Mary were led into a meeting room, where they finally found their son. He was surrounded by the old priests of the Temple, called Pharisees and Sadducees, asking them questions about God and about the promises of a future King. The temple priests were also asking him questions and astonished to hear the young boy answer difficult questions about the Law and the history of the Israelites.

When Jesus noticed that his parents were in the room watching him, he ran over to them and gave them both a big hug. Mary was crying tears of joy for finding him. Joseph began to scold Jesus for running off and being separated from the rest of their group. Mary asked him "Why did you run off. We were both so worried that we would never find you."

Jesus looked at his parents and told them, "Dad, Mom, don't you realize that I should be doing what my Father told me to do?" To this, they didn't fully understand what he meant, because he was talking about God, but they were very glad to have him back. So, they returned to Nazareth

Jesus continued to grow into a young man and then an adult as an assistant to his father in the carpenter's shop, helping his mother, being a part of the community, going to the synagogue every weekend, being friends to others. He went to the classes where he and all the other children of the town learned from the old scrolls about Abraham and Moses and all the prophets, and the rise and fall of the Jewish people into different evil kings. And so, he grew up with everyone thinking that he was a wonderful young man.

5. Jesus Is Baptized

After being baptized, Jesus came up immediately from the water; and behold, the heavens were opened, and he saw the Spirit of God descending like a dove and lighting on Him, and behold, a voice out of the heavens said, "This is My Beloved Son, in whom I am well-pleased."
(Matthew 3:16-17)

Jesus grew to become a young man of thirty years old, finally accepted as a mature adult in the eyes of the Jewish community. He had heard that his cousin John was becoming quite a celebrity around the country. John had gone out into the desert for months, living on what God provided for him. He wore an animal skin, tied with a leather belt, and lived on nothing but locusts and honey.

When he returned from the desert, he began to travel all over the country, teaching about a coming King. Some people even thought that John was the Messiah they had been looking for. But John told them that he was only the forerunner of the Messiah, that he wasn't even worthy to tie the shoes of the person coming after him.

The people of Israel had been spiritually dead for hundreds of years. The last prophet before John the Baptist was named Malachi. Malachi prophesied that "I will send you a messenger, and he will prepare the way for the Lord." But for four hundred years there hadn't been a real prophet in Israel. John preached about the coming Messiah, calling the people of his time a "generation of snakes".

He also told people that God was telling him they should be baptized in the Jordan River, to signify to God their return to worshipping him. John baptized with water but taught that soon a new king would arise who baptized with the Holy Spirit. People began to follow him around, to listen to him teaching about all the old prophets who had promised that someday a new King of Israel would come along and that this king was near. At that moment, John didn't realize that it was his own cousin Jesus he was prophesying about.

God told Jesus to go find John, and he found out where John was and went down to the Jordan River. He sat in the grass and listened to John preaching to a crowd around him about God and all the miracles that God had done for Israel over the centuries, and about their need to return to God. When John was done preaching, he offered to baptize anyone who wanted to come forward.

Jesus stood up and walked toward him, and John saw his cousin coming and smiled. They hugged each other, and Jesus told John, "I would like to be baptized." John looked at Jesus and told him, "No, cousin, you should be baptizing me!"

Jesus looked deep into John's eyes and told him, "Dear John, there will come a time that I will be able to baptize—but right now is your time, and it's in front of God's eyes that you are to fulfill your destiny so that I might be able to later fulfill mine."

So, John led him out into the river and helped to submerge Jesus into the water. When Jesus stood up, water dripped off his hair and his chin and his clothes, they saw what looked like a white dove coming down from heaven and landed on Jesus's head and disappeared. Then everyone in the crowd heard a loud voice coming above that said, "This is my beloved Son, in whom I am well pleased."

The crowd was astonished. John and Jesus looked at each other and smiled, and then John hugged Jesus tightly. At the moment that the spirit landed upon Jesus, he was able to communicate directly with God and begin his own righteous ministry.

From then on, John would teach to all his followers that his cousin Jesus was the "Lamb of God, who would take away all the sins of the world." He told his followers that they should be ready to follow this Jesus instead of him because Jesus surely was the Son of God.

6. Jesus Chooses His Apostles

Now as Jesus was walking by the Sea of Galilee, He saw two brothers, Simon who was called Peter, and Andrew his brother, casting a net into the sea; for they were fishermen. And He said to them, "Follow Me, and I will make you fishers of men."
(Matthew 4:18-19)

God led Jesus into the desert and lived there for forty days, praying about the ministry that he was to begin, working in his mind all the scriptures about his future and about all thing things he had learned growing up. Near the end of that time, Satan, the devil, came to Jesus and tried to tempt him to not start his ministry. He tempted Jesus with food first because Jesus had been living in the desert so long. He tried to trick Jesus into thinking he could jump off a high cliff and that God would send angels to save him. Then, the devil told him he could make him the King of the World, richer beyond his wildest imagination—if he would only worship the Devil. The devil could do this honestly because Adam had given him the control of the whole world and all its riches when Adam sinned. Jesus answered every temptation with the Word of God—and eventually, the Devil backed off and went away.

Now, after Jesus returned from the desert, God told him that he needed a team to work with him. He began to look around for people that could follow him and learn from him. He knew that he would have a lot of followers, who he could teach about God and God's will for man, but he needed some special people around him to whom he could teach the deeper secrets of God, and who would carry on his words after he was gone.

He met two of John's followers, who believed what John had taught about Jesus. Jesus asked, "Why are you following me?"

The men answered, "Where do you live? We want to come to hear more about God from you." The two men followed Jesus to his house, and it was already late afternoon, so they ate and talked about God all night. The next morning, one of the men, whose name was Andrew, told Jesus that he wanted to go find his brother, who would love to hear all about God too.

Andrew went to Jesus' house with his brother Simon. Jesus told him that he would call Simon by the name of Cephas, which was Peter in English and meant a tiny little pebble. Peter was a man full of emotions, he would be a strong believer one day, and a coward the next. One day, he was bound to forsake Jesus. That was why Jesus called him Peter because he would blow hot one day, and cold the next day. Andrew and Peter and another disciple stayed with Jesus all day, talking about wonderful things.

The next day, Jesus began by leaving his house one morning in Nazareth, and taking a peaceful walk to Lake Kinnereth, talking to God and his three new friends along the way. It was a beautiful day, with a soft breeze blowing over the lake. Fishing boats bobbed up and down on the little ripples of the lake, and many boats were already out in the middle of the lake with their fishermen.

The four of them walked together along the seashore and saw a group of people in a boat close to shore. Everyone knew each other in this little fishing town, so Jesus recognized the fisherman Zebedee, and his two sons James and John, and some servants who were helping them. They were busy fixing holes that had torn in their fishing webs. Jesus asked for their attention, and so they rowed back to the shore and talked with James and John about God, too. They told Zebedee that they were going off with Jesus to talk about God, and Zebedee allowed them to go.

They came to the next little fishing village, called Bethsaida, which was where Andrew and Peter's house was. One of the brothers ran to find a friend he had, named Philip. Philip was so excited to hear about God and saw how happy his friends were with Jesus. So, he ran off to find another friend of theirs, whose name was Nathaniel.

One by one, Jesus found friends who would not only be followers of his words, disciples but be fully committed to Jesus and to whom he could teach the innermost secret of God. Those he called apostles, and there were twelve of them. Because these men already deeply believed in God, Jesus was able to trust them and teach them the deeper mysteries about God. For the common people, he could only teach them the basics, which they could understand. They were Peter, Andrew, Matthew, James, Phillip, Thomas, John, ... Bartholomew, James the son of Alpheus, Simon Zelotes, Jude the brother of James, and Judas Iscariot. The first eleven of these men all came from the Galilee region, but Judas came from a town named Kerioth, close to the Mediterranean Sea.

7. Water into Wine

Jesus said to them, "Fill the waterpots with water." So they filled them up to the brim. And He said to them, "Draw some out now and take it to the headwaiter." So they took it to him. When the headwaiter tasted the water, which had become wine
(John 2:7-9)

After he had assembled his team, Jesus began to visit all the Jewish places of worship called synagogues around the Galilee to preach. When he went to the synagogue in his own town, Nazareth, it was his turn to read from the scrolls. That was a practice then—each man took turns to read from a scroll every week.

Jesus read from the scroll of Isaiah:

The Spirit of the Lord GOD is upon me
Because the LORD has anointed me
To bring good news to the afflicted;
He has sent me to bind up the brokenhearted,
To proclaim liberty to captives
And freedom to prisoners;
To proclaim the favorable year of the LORD
(Isaiah 61:1-2)

This statement from the prophecy of Isaiah was a good summary of what his whole ministry was going to be about. Jesus stopped before the end of the verse, which said, "and the day of vengeance of our God" because that was only yet to come.

One day, Jesus was invited to a large nuptial in the nearby village of Cana. Jesus's mother, Mary, was also invited to the party. Weddings in those days were large, joyous occasions that often lasted several days, and included a lot of food and wine.

Sometime during the party, Mary approached Jesus to tell him they'd run out of wine. He first told his mother that it wasn't his responsibility to get more wine, because it wasn't his wedding, but they told her that he would fix it anyway. Mary went over to the men who were serving all the guests, and pointed to her son Jesus and told them, "My son can help, do whatever he tells you to do."

Then Jesus walked over to the servants and told them to go get six big clay pots and fill them up to the very top with water. Jesus talked to God and when God told him it was ok, Jesus told the head servant to dip a cup into one of the pots and fill a cup and take it to the father of the bride. The servant did as he was asked, and the father sipped the water, which had turned into the most splendid wine. Nobody except the servants knew that the pots had only been filled with water, not wine.

The father of the bride called over the bridegroom, his new son-in-law, and told the crowd that they had all started off drinking the lesser wine, but now the finest wine was in the room. He did not know it, but the father of the bride was really talking about Jesus, the real fine wine in the room! This was the first of the miracles that Jesus would perform in his ministry.

8. Jesus Calms the Storm

He said to them, "Why are you afraid, you men of little faith?" Then He got up and rebuked the winds and the sea, and it became perfectly calm. The men were amazed, and said, "What kind of a man is this, that even the winds and the sea obey Him?"
(Matthew 8:26-27)

O ne day, Jesus and his apostles had been teaching large crowds of people around the city of Capernaum, a city much bigger than his hometown of Nazareth, which was also alongside the Sea of Kinnereth. Jesus went to the synagogue and preached there about the deliverance of God with great power.

A possessed man came out from the crowd. The devil has thousands of devil spirits under him, who are able to possess the minds of many who are not given to God. God originally created the angels and put three angels in charge of them, Michael, Gabriel, and Lucifer. Michael was the angel who fights for Gods people. Gabriel was the angel who brings great messages to people. Lucifer was created to be the Angel of Light. When the angel Lucifer revolted against God, thinking he was as good as God, God cast him down to the earth and Lucifer acquired a third of his fellows when he was cast to the earth.

"How you have fallen from heaven,
O star of the morning, son of the dawn!
You have been cut down to the earth,
You who have weakened the nations!
But you said in your heart,
'I will ascend to heaven;
I will raise my throne above the stars of God,
And I will sit on the mount of assembly
In the recesses of the north.
'I will ascend above the heights of the clouds;
I will make myself like the Most High.
Nevertheless you will be thrust down to Sheol,

To the recesses of the pit.
(Isaiah 14:12-15)

God is only perfect Love. He doesn't hurt or kill anyone. But the devil only lies, kills and destroys. The devil's angels worship the devil like he was God, and they followed his orders around the earth. They are the ones who hurt and kill, to make them sick and die, who make men do evil things.

The possessed man boldly walked up to Jesus and said, "Leave us alone Jesus. Are you here to destroy us? I know who you are, the Holy One of God." The man didn't know who Jesus was, but the devil spirit inside him did. Jesus demanded the departure of the bad element—and so it immediately did, and the man was healed of the torment the spirit was putting him through. God's spirit working through people who believe him are much more powerful than these evil spirits, and if they are ordered to leave someone, they have to go.

The people in the synagogue were astonished to see a man with such power. Word was spread around Capernaum, and many people came to see him and hear his words. They brought many sick people with them, and Jesus was able to call upon God to heal them all. It was a wonderful time, with people smiling and hugging each other seeing the many miracles that Jesus performed.

His apostle, Peter, asked Jesus to come to his house there because his mother was sick. The crowd followed Jesus and his apostles down the street and then stood outside while Jesus and the twelve apostles went into the house. Jesus went over to the lady, and held her hands, and prayed for her, and she was immediately healed. She felt so perfect that she got up and began cooking dinner for all of them.

The crowd of people kept calling for Jesus to come back out, and when he did, he saw it had grown larger, and many other sick people were there hoping to be healed. Jesus taught and healed them for many hours until it was dark.

Jesus was getting tired, but the crowd just kept growing and growing. Jesus told one of his apostles to go find a boat to borrow, so they could get away from the crowd and get a little rest. A boat was found, and they all climbed aboard it, and Jesus fell deeply asleep.

Suddenly, in the middle of the lake, and far from any shore, a strong wind came up, and the waves increased, and the boat began to rock up and down. Water splashed into the bottom of the boat. The apostles were scared, thinking the boat would tip over and they would all drown, but Jesus was peacefully sleeping.

They got so scared, they finally shook Jesus until he woke up. They told him, "Jesus, Jesus, help us. We are all going to die out here!"

Jesus looked at them and shook his head. They had just seen all sorts of people be healed the day before, and now they are all scared. "Why are you afraid. Oh, ye of little faith", he said to them." They still didn't really believe that God could do anything.

The Jesus walked over to the edge of the boat and bowed his head and prayed to God. Immediately the wind stopped, and the sea became calm again. The men shook their heads in amazement, whispering to each other, "What kind of man is that, that ever the winds and the sea obey him." Jesus just smiled and them and went back to bed.

Jesus continued touring around Galilee, preaching and teaching and healing the sick. But he also had caught the attention of the religious leaders of the day, who began to question if a man had the right to forgive sins, to heal the sick, and so on. They were afraid because of the obvious power of God that Jesus demonstrated.

In those days, the priests really didn't love God

or follow Him. They lived well off the donations that people paid to the Temple and objected to anyone who might threaten to take away their easy life. There were two main groups of priests, called the Pharisees and the Sadducees. They made up all sorts of silly rules for the people to follow, which were not really based on the old prophets. They told people what they could and could not eat, or wear, or do, but it was all just to control them. Many times in the ministry of Jesus, he told them that they were sinning against God, because they were supposed to be helping the people but were really only using them.

9. Sermon on the Mount

*When Jesus saw the crowds, He went up
on the mountain; and after He sat down, His
disciples came to Him. He opened His mouth
and began to teach them...*
(Matthew 5:1-2)

After he began preaching all around the region of Galilee, where Nazareth was, more and more people began to travel from all over the country to hear him. He taught large crowds in the synagogues of the Jews, who met every Saturday. He taught crowds in the markets, on the streets, and people in their homes. Soon, people started to come from as far away as Jerusalem and even from across Jordan River and in other countries to hear him speak and to watch his miracles.

One day, a massive crowd formed that was so big

that people in the back couldn't even see or hear what was happening. Jesus told them all to follow him, and he left the city he was in and walked to a high hill, where he could stand above all the people and they could all see and hear him. Jesus stood, but everyone sat down in the grass and stared at him.

Jesus began to preach of all the things of God, in a loving but firm way. He began by setting forth general guidelines or rules for people to follow, so they could find Godly happiness in their lives:

"Blessed are the poor in spirit, for theirs is the kingdom of heaven.

Blessed are those who mourn, for they shall be comforted.

Blessed are the gentle, for they shall inherit the earth.

Blessed are those who hunger and thirst for righteousness, for they shall be satisfied. Blessed are the merciful, for they shall receive mercy.

Blessed are the pure in heart, for they shall see

God.

Blessed are the peacemakers, for they shall be called sons of God.

Blessed are those who have been persecuted for the sake of righteousness, for theirs is the kingdom of heaven.

Blessed are you when people insult you and persecute you, and falsely say all kinds of evil against you because of Me.

Rejoice and be glad, for your reward in heaven is great; for, in the same way, they persecuted the prophets who were before you."

(Matthew 5:2-12)

Then Jesus continued all day, speaking for hours about the Laws of Moses, and the Ten Commandments, and how people had twisted the laws to make them all easier to get past. Jesus taught them to be peaceful, and loving, forgiving even someone who was mean to you. Jesus told them to let their light shine for the whole world to see it.

Jesus' teachings were different from the angry words of the ministers who taught in the synagogues, who were often mad and taught people to fear and hate. Jesus's words were so much kinder and made God seem to them more as a loving God—than a God who made people sick or die.

He also scolded people who stand out in the street corners, praying for everyone to see how important they think they are, and told them to instead go into a closet and talk to God person to person. He even taught them an example of a prayer to say, just between them and God:

"Our Father who is in heaven,
Hallowed be Your name.
Your kingdom come.
Your will be done,
On earth as it is in heaven.
Give us this day our daily bread.
And forgive us our debts, as we also have
forgiven our debtors.

And do not lead us into temptation, but deliver us from evil. For Yours are the kingdom and the power and the glory forever. Amen."
(Matthew 6:9-13)

By the end of the day, everyone was smiling and hugging and some were even crying, having learned that they were listening to a man who spoke directly from God's heart.

10. Jesus Forgives and Heals a Paralyzed Man

And they came, bringing to Him a paralytic, carried by four men. Being unable to get to Him because of the crowd, they removed the roof above Him; and when they had dug an opening, they let down the pallet on which the paralytic was lying. And Jesus seeing their faith said to the paralytic, "Son, your sins are forgiven.

(Mark 2:3-6)

Jesus and his apostles went back to the town of Capernaum again—and soon, another large crowd had assembled around the house he was at. So many people came to hear him preach to the point that the whole house was filled, and people pushed into all the doors and the windows of the house to hear him.

While he was preaching, four men came to the house with a bed carrying another man. This man was paralyzed, and he couldn't walk or even talk. His friends wanted him to be healed by Jesus, but they couldn't even get close enough to the house to hear him, let alone get to Jesus and hope that he can heal their friend.

In those days, many of the houses had flat roofs, covered over with wood and straw. One of the men suggested that they go on the roof, open up a part it, right above where Jesus was standing. They got some rope and tied it to the four corners of the bed, and with each person holding onto a corner, lowered the bed right down from the roof and it rested right in front of Jesus.

Jesus looked up at the four men and smiled. He was amazed they people believed in him so much to go to all this trouble to see their friend healed.

He looked at the man on the bed, and bend down to look him in the eyes, and he told him "Son, thy sins are forgiven."

But there were in the crowd before him from the synagogue, and they began to whisper between themselves, "How can this man forgive sins, only God can do that." God told Jesus what they were whispering, and stared at them in the crowd. He said, "Why do you doubt the power of God to do anything. Is it easier for me to say, 'Your sins are forgiven', or just 'Take up your bed and walk?' Because God can do anything, he has given the Son of God to act as God on the earth and forgive sins."

Just looked back to him then uttered, "Get up off your bed, and go home." He was cured of paralysis almost instantly, and he jumped up to hug Jesus, crying and thanking him. He got his bed, and pushed his way through the crowd, as people were smiling and hugging him with joy. Astonished, they said, "Wow, we have never ever seen anything like that before."

11. The Faith of the Centurion

And when Jesus entered Capernaum, a centurion came to Him, imploring Him, and saying, "Lord, my servant is lying paralyzed at home, fearfully tormented." Jesus said to him, "I will come and heal him."
(Matthew 8:5-7)

After Jesus was done preaching to the people, a man in a soldier's uniform knocked on his door. He was what was called a centurion, an officer in the Roman army, who had a hundred soldiers following his orders. Jesus invited him in, and the man asked Jesus, "Can you help my servant? He is paralyzed and is very sick and suffering." Perhaps he had heard about the other paralyzed man that Jesus had healed.

Jesus told him, "Sure, I'll come to heal him."

The officer said, "Jesus, I am a worthy that you should even walk into my house. I am a Roman officer, and when I tell my soldiers to march, they do it. When I say to fight, they do it. I have heard you teaching and seen some of your miracles. I have heard of many other things that I wasn't there for, but I believe in everything that you say and do is from God."

Jesus was amazed to hear by a Roman soldier because Jesus was sent to the Jewish people, not to the Romans. They, as well as everyone else who wasn't Jewish, were called Gentiles in the scrolls of God. He wasn't sent to the Gentiles, but there was one who believed totally in what Jesus said and did.

"Jesus, if you just come and heal him, I will believe it."

Jesus had not even seen such believing in the

Jewish people. They all could believe if they saw him perform a miracle, but nobody had yet believed him enough to just believe his words. He told the centurion, that lots of people will come from all over, Jews and Gentiles, but many of even the Jewish people who think they know God will find out someday that they did not due to their refusal to believe the things Jesus said and did. "Since you have believed, even though you aren't Jewish, God sees your believing, and your servant will be healed, ". That hour, the servant of the centurion began to feel better and was healed of all his illness.

Then Jesus left Capernaum and when to a small town called Nain, with his apostles and a large crowd of worshippers following him. There Jesus encountered a burial party, carrying the body of a boy. Most of the little town was following the body. Crying loudly was a widow woman, the dead boy's mother, who had lost her only son. Jesus told her, "Don't cry," and touched him and uttered, "Young man, I say to you 'Arise'", then immediately he rose! Again, many who saw Jesus and knew that the boy was really dead, believed that he was performing miracles.

12. Feeding the Crowd

And He took the five loaves and the two fishes—
and looking up toward heaven, He blessed the
food and broke the loaves and He kept
giving them to the disciples to set before them;
and He divided up the two fish among them all.
They all ate and were satisfied.
(Mark 6:41-42)

J esus decided it was time to send out his apostles into different cities so that they could see that they, too, had the spirit of God on them and that they could do the same miracles that Jesus did. He paired them up into six teams and sent them to six different towns. Jesus told them to not take any money or food with them; to not bring any extra clothes with them, either; and to instead let God take care of them along the way.

Jesus also taught them, "Don't worry when you find people who don't believe you. Just shake the dust off your feet and go somewhere else. They can learn about God, and if they don't want to hear, they will have to face the consequences before God someday. It's not your fault if people don't want to believe, it is just your job to speak the truth and let them believe what they want to believe."

The men went out as Jesus had said, and when people heard that they were the apostles of Jesus, they invited them into their houses and feed them and gave them beds to sleep on, so that the men would teach them about Jesus. These six teams went and performed many of the miracles that they had seen Jesus perform, and soon crowds began to follow them as well. They taught the people many of what Jesus shared about God.

Upon returning to Jesus, they were all bubbling with excitement. They all told Jesus of all the wonderful things they have learned and seen, and the miracles that they had performed. Jesus was pleased to see that they learned how loving God is, that God answers prayers if you only believed in Him.

Jesus knew they were tired and asked them to go into a quiet place in the desert, where they could all rest for a while. But the crowds followed them, and soon they were all surrounded by many people. Around 5 thousand people were surrounding them—men, women, and children of all ages. He taught them all day long about God and about how God loves them all and wants to be with them.

When it started getting close to nighttime, the apostles told Jesus that he should let these people find some dinner in the nearby villages. They complained that they didn't have hundreds of dollars to go buy food for all the people.

When the day got late, Jesus asked his apostles,

how much food do you have?

The apostles told him that they only had 2 cooked fishes and 5 loaves of bread. Jesus took the food and told everyone to sit down. They sat down around him in crowds of fifty and groups of a hundred. Jesus took the bread and the fish and prayed that God consecrated the food and divided the bread to smaller pieces and the fish into smaller pieces, and he gave each of his disciples a piece of bread and a piece of fish in the bottom of a basket.

The apostles, just back from sccing themselves perform so many miracles, took the baskets and started passing out pieces of bread and fish from them. Every time they reached into their basket, there were more and more bread and fish in them.

The people surrounded them ate happily, and when dinner was all over, each of the apostles still had baskets full of chunks of bread and fish leftover, even after all five thousand people in the crowd had gotten their fill, both of the bread and fish, and of the word of God.

13. Jesus Walks on Water

And in the fourth watch of the night, He came to them, walking on the sea. When the disciples saw Him walking on the sea, they were terrified, and said, "It is a ghost!" And they cried out in fear. But immediately Jesus spoke to them, saying, "Take courage, it is I; do not be afraid."
(Matthew 14:25-27)

After Jesus had fed the five thousand people, he sent them all home and told his apostles that he wanted to be alone, too. He told them to go rent a boat and go back over the lake to Galilee so that he could spend some time praying to God. Jesus went up into a mountain and watched the sun going down and stared at the beauty of all the stars in heaven. He stayed up all night, praying to God and remembering all the things that had happened to him.

About 3 o'clock in the morning, God told Jesus that his apostles were in trouble and that they needed to be rescued. Jesus immediately departed then headed to the lake and saw that a storm had come in. The wind was very strong, and white caps roll across the water of the lake.

In the middle of the lake, on their rented boat, the apostles were once again being tossed to and fro, up and down, fearing for their lives. The last time, Jesus was with them and he calmed the waters, but this time they were alone. They were very afraid and cried and screamed as the boat rolled back and forth, and big waves splashed water into the boat.

Jesus began to walk across the water, and although his sandals got wet from the waves, Jesus didn't sink. He kept walking until he got close to the boat. The men in the boat saw him coming through the spray of the water and thought they were seeing a ghost walking towards them. They became even more afraid than they were. They thought they were all going to die, right then and there.

But Jesus called out, and said, "Be happy, don't be afraid. It's me!" The men were amazed and very glad that Jesus had come to them. Peter, who was the most afraid of all of them, called out to Jesus to let him walk on water towards him because he just couldn't wait for one more second to be next to Jesus and out of the rocking boat.

Jesus called to Peter, and he stood upright on the lake. Even Peter was shocked. He began to walk towards Jesus, and as long as he stared directly at him, he walked on the top of the water. He got closer and closer to Jesus. But he turned and looked at the boat, now far away and rolling around the in water, and he began to slowly sink. The water covered his toes, and then his knees. He looked back at Jesus and cried, "Jesus, Jesus, save me!"

Jesus reached out and grabbed Peter's hand, and Peter rose up to the top of the water again. Jesus scolded him, "You didn't believe in me, you looked back at the world instead of keeping focused on God to save you."

Then Jesus and Peter walked hand in hand across the water and climbed into the boat with the other apostles. As soon as Jesus stood in the boat, the wind stopped, and the sea began to calm down. The men all around him were amazed once more with all they had seen and said, "You really are the Son of God."

Jesus continued around Galilee, teaching everywhere he went. On one occasion, he told the people that the Word of God was like a farmer throwing seeds out into a planted field. Some of the seeds fell onto stones and dried up in the sun without sprouting. Some fell into the weeds, and they started to grow, but they got choked up by all the weeds. But some fell into the dirt and grew up big and strong. He explained that this was like the Word of God; some refuse to accept it, so these people don't even get the chance to grow. Others hear it, but they refuse to avoid earth's pleasures, so what Word they heard was soon choked out, but some will hear the Word and grow and spread it to others.

He also taught them about the future in a parable. Now, when Jesus taught, he used a lot of what is called, "parables." He could teach his apostles many deep truths about God, but when he was teaching crowds of people he mostly spoke in the form of parables—which is like a fable, a story with a meaning to it in the end, if you think about it. Jesus usually taught about the farmers and fishermen and the world that everyone knew about, in simple words, so everyone could understand him.

Jesus said that when a farmer gathers together his crops, he doesn't try to root out all the weeds first. He gathers both the crop and the weeds together, and sorts out the good food, and burns up all the weeds. This he was talking about man, that God will someday separate out all the good crops from the weeds, and the weeds will be destroyed.

14. The Transfiguration

*Six days later, Jesus took with Him Peter
and James and John, and brought them up on a
high mountain by themselves. And He was
transfigured before them; and His garments
became radiant and exceedingly white, as no
launderer on earth can whiten them.*
(Mark 9:2-3)

One fine day, as Jesus and his apostles were going around the region of Galilee, Jesus asked John, James, and Peter for them to follow him up into a high mountain. Jesus didn't tell them why, but they were obedient and climbed up the mountain behind him.

When they reached the top of the mountain, Jesus began to glow with a heavenly light. His robe, which was a common brown color used throughout the area, glowed whiter than any white the three apostles had ever seen.

Then Moses and Elishia appeared on either side of Jesus. They glowed with the same heavenly glow and the same brilliant pure white. Above them, a white glowing cloud stopped right over them, and even though the other clouds were moving by in the wind, this one special cloud stayed put. Jesus talked quietly with the two angels beside him about things of God to come.

The apostles became worried and dumbfounded. One of them said, "Jesus, let us take some rocks and make three monuments, one for you and one of both Moses and Elishia." They thought they were doing something good, but they were really just there to witness the events. Then, from the cloud, a mysterious voice emerged, saying, "This is my beloved son; hear him."

The three apostles looked down from the cloud and saw Jesus was standing alone again. The heavenly glow was gone, and Moses and Elishia had vanished.

Upon going down, Jesus asked his apostles to keep what just happened as a secret until he rose—but the men failed to comprehend Jesus.

At that time, Jesus had not taught about his impending death. They thought Jesus would somehow conquer the Romans, take over the country, and rule as the King. They still believed this even up until Jesus said his last words to them.

Jesus knew at that moment, after hearing the whispered promises from Moses and Elishia, that to fulfill all the promises of God, it was to become necessary that he was going to die, but to not be afraid, because God would raise him up again in three days' time. To salvage humankind, he'd have to agonize all the things that the devil was able to throw at him because the devil had always thrown the same things on mankind. But it was Jesus's secret at that moment, and he couldn't tell the apostles because they could not yet understand it.

15. Jesus and the Children

Then some children were brought to Him so that He might lay His hands on them and pray, and the disciples rebuked them. But Jesus said, "Let the children alone, and do not hinder them from coming to Me; for the kingdom of heaven belongs to such as these."
(Matthew 19:13-14)

J esus loved children most of all because they were innocent and so willing to accept love and anything positive. Jesus often used children as an example in his teachings because all they wanted was love and to be taught wonderful things. The Bible used the words "child" or "children" 763 times throughout the Bible.

He taught them that children were the easiest to bring into the Kingdom of Heaven. Now, the

Kingdom of Heaven is not a physical place in heaven itself, but it's a walk on the earth of a person who loves and believes and trusts God. Everyone has a choice to live their life according to God and Jesus and when somebody does that, they can see wondrous miracles in their lives and develop a one-to-one relationship with God.

Then Jesus and his apostles began a trip. They left the region of Galilee, walking to the east, and crossed over the Jordan River.

The religious leaders of the Jews, called Pharisees, came to Jesus to try to trick him into saying something against God. They invented several tricky questions, but Jesus was smarter than all of them and answered every question in such a way that they couldn't accuse him of saying anything wrong.

Then, a group of children was brought to Jesus, even though his disciples questioned why Jesus was blessing babies.

"Permit the children to come to Me, and do not hinder them, for the kingdom of God belongs to such as these. Truly I say to you, whoever does not receive the kingdom of God like a child will not enter it at all."
(Luke 18:16-17)

About this time a man named Jarius came to Jesus to ask for help. Jarius was a ruler in a synagogue in Galilee and he had seen Jesus perform many miracles. Jarius told Jesus that his twelve-year-old daughter, Tabitha, was very sick, close to the point of dying. "Please come to my house and heal her, so she may live," Jarius asked.

On the way, Jesus was followed by a large crowd, and they encountered a cursed woman and couldn't go to worship in the synagogue because of it for twelve years. She believed that healing would come by touching Jesus's robes. When the woman did, He felt the blessing of God going through him, and stopped and turned to the woman and said Who touched my clothes?" The woman admitted she did and told him she thought she could be healed just by touching his clothing. Jesus saw her believing, and said, "Your believing has made you whole."

Jesus continued walking down the street, and men from the synagogue came running up to tell Jesus that Jarius' daughter had just died, and he didn't have to go there now. He told them, "Don't be scared, only believe."

When Jesus got to the house of Jarius, and went into the little girl's bedroom, and said, "Tabitha, wake up." And she did! All the people were astonished at the miracle, but Jesus simply told Jarius to cook something for the girl, because she was hungry.

Jesus always knew that innocent young children were like empty glasses, able to be filled up with whatever their parents put in them. If they were raised with hate and anger and fear, that is how they would live their lives. But if they were filled with love and peace, and the love of a God who cares for them always, they would live their lives that way. Even the old prophets had written that "If you raise up your child according to the Word of God, they will return to it." God didn't promise that they wouldn't stay away from God, but that that foundation would become the bedrock of their lives.

16. The Good Samaritan

But a Samaritan, who was on a journey, came
upon him; and when he saw him, he felt
compassion, and came to him and bandaged up
his wounds, pouring oil and wine on them; and
he put him on his own beast, and brought him to
an inn and took care of him.
(Luke 10:33-34)

J esus continued to teach parables to the people who surrounded him. One of his parables was about the mustard seed. The mustard is a bush, and it produces seeds that are so very tiny to the point that you can hardly see them. Jesus said that faith or believing is a little one of these little tiny seeds because all you need to have faith in is the truth that everything is possible with God, the Creator. All you need to do is ask and believe in God—and you can move mountains.

One day a man came to Jesus who was trained to study the laws of Moses and to teach the laws to others. He had been sent by the Pharisees to try to trick Jesus, and he asked Jesus directly, "What shall I do to get eternal life?

Instead of answering, Jesus replied, "Well, you study the law of Moses. What do YOU think it says?"

The lawyer said, "Well, Moses wrote to love God with all your heart, and with all your soul, and with all your strength, and love your neighbor as yourself."

He was correct, Jesus said. But then the lawyer asked, "And who is my neighbor?"

Instead of answering the man's question, he began to tell him a parable. Jesus said that a man went south from Jerusalem to Jericho and was attacked and robbed by bandits along the way. They stole his money and his clothes, beat him up, and wounded him on the side of the road.

A synagogue priest came down the street and saw the wounded man on the side of the road, went just across the road and passed him without stopping to see if he could help. Another man, called a Levite, which was a priest who worked in the great Temple in Jerusalem, came by and he also saw the man but just kept riding.

Then came along a Samaritan. Now, the people of Samaria were really not liked by the Jews, because they were poor people who had been imported into the country from the country of Babylon long ago when the Judeans were taken into captivity hundreds of years before. But this man was kind, and went over to the injured man, and wrapped bandages around where he was bleeding, and washed him up with oil and water. Then he helped the man get up onto his horse and drove him to an inn. He rented a room, and cared for the wounded man, bringing him food and water and changing his bandages for him.

The next day, he paid the innkeeper some money and asked that he care for the wounded man until he came back, and he would pay him more when he got back.

When Jesus finished the story, he asked the lawyer, "Now, of the three on the road, the synagogue rabbi, the Temple priest, or the Samaritan who everyone hated, which do you say is the wounded man's neighbor?"

The lawyer looked at Jesus and said, "His neighbor was the one who showed mercy to him."

Jesus uttered, "Go and do so likewise." Hence, what can be learned from this parable is that no matter who you are—rich or poor, smart or foolish—it doesn't matter to God even if you are one of the priests in the Temple, God knows when you love another and when you don't, so love everyone.

17. Mary and Martha

Now as they were traveling along, He entered a village; and a woman named Martha welcomed Him into her home. She had a sister called Mary, who was seated at the Lord's feet, listening to His word.
(Luke 10:38-39)

Now, after the lawyer went away, Jesus continued walking and came into a small village called Bethany and ran into a woman named Martha. Bethany was nestled in the hills east of Jerusalem, about two miles away. Martha didn't really know who Jesus was, but she invited Jesus to come into her house and have dinner. It was normal for people in those days to invite strangers into their houses and to feed them and give them a place to rest from their journeys.

Martha had a sister, named Mary. Now, Mary had heard of this Jesus, maybe she had even seen him preaching, and she sat Jesus in a chair and she sat on the floor to talk to him. She washed the dust-off Jesus' feet and massaged them with a special expensive rare oil. She even dried his feet with her long hair! This was an act of honor to a special guest in those days.

Martha was inside the kitchen, preparing a meal, and because she didn't know who Jesus was, got upset with her sister for just sitting on the floor while she did all the work. She came into the room and asked Jesus "Can you tell Mary to come to help me cooking, instead of sitting there talking to you?"

Jesus looked at Martha, and said to her, "Martha, Martha, you are all upset with your sister and upset about a bunch of other things, but your sister is going the most important thing she could be doing, by talking to me instead of helping you."

At some point, the women must have sent for their brother, whose name was Lazarus, although he isn't mentioned specifically. He becomes important later in the story but became a good friend of Jesus. Later, Jesus would spend a lot of time together with Mary and Martha and Lazarus in Bethany.

Afterward, Jesus went into Jerusalem to celebrate the holiday of Hanukkah, which is sometimes referred to as Feast of Lights. This holiday celebrated the recovery of the Temple from the Greeks after it had been captured and miss used. Jesus was called in front of the Temple priests again, and he taught some things that tied directly to the holiday they were celebrating:

"I am the Light of the world; he who follows Me will not walk in the darkness, but will have the Light of life." So the Pharisees said to Him, "You are testifying about Yourself; Your testimony is not true." Jesus answered and said to

them, "Even if I testify about Myself, My testimony is true, for I know where I came from and where I am going, but you do not know where I come from or where I going. You judge according to the flesh; I am not judging anyone. But even if I do judge, My judgment is true; for I am not alone in it, but I and the Father who sent Me.

(John 8:12-16)

Later, Jesus was teaching his own followers when he told them, "If you continue in My word, then you are truly disciples of Mine; and you will know the truth, and the truth will make you free."

18. The Lost Sheep

So He told them this parable, saying, "What man among you if he has a hundred sheep and has lost one of them, does not leave the ninety-nine in the open pasture and go after the one which is lost until he finds it? When he has found it, he lays it on his shoulders, rejoicing.
(Luke 15:3-5)

After the Feast of Dedication, Jesus and his apostles traveled through southern Judea, and the Bible records him teaching many parables to the people during this trip. One of Jesus's parables that he used to teach in various ways was about the lost sheep. He used the same parable elsewhere about the lost coin, or the lost son—all of which have the same ending.

Jesus was teaching a group of common people

from the countryside. The religious leaders watched the sermon he gave, complaining that they were the smart religious people, but this man Jesus was always hanging out with a much of sinners. They thought that if he such an important man to God, that he should be spending all his time with the religious leaders. But they wouldn't have believed anything he said, so Jesus preferred to be around people who might be able to learn from him.

Jesus told the crowd that God was like a shepherd that had a hundred sheep, but one of them got lost in the hills. So, the shepherd left his flock with other shepherds, and went out and searched and searched and searched, until he found the lost sheep. He hugged it and led it back to the rest of the flock where it could be fed and protected from wild animals. He was happy that most of his sheep were content to stay where they were safe, but even happier when one strayed away and came back to him.

Then he told them the story of a lost coin. In those days, when a woman got married, she adorned her hair with ten special silver coins, which had hooks attached to them, passed from mother to daughter over generations. When a woman lost one of these coins, she thought that her family would be forever cursed. The woman told her girlfriends, and then swept and cleaned every inch of her house until she found the missing coin. She told all her girlfriends, and they all rejoiced with her that the jewelry was found, and the family wouldn't be cursed. The moral of these stories is that we were all lost to God, and God is overjoyed when we find our ways back to Him.

19. The Lost Son

*And he said to him, 'Son, you have always been
with me, and all that is mine is yours. But we
had to celebrate and rejoice, for this brother of
yours was dead and has begun to live
and was lost and has been found."*
(Luke 15:31-32)

Then, Jesus continued and told them about a lost son. A man had two sons, and the younger one asked him if he could have all his inheritance. Hence, the man took half of his money and gave it to the younger son, and the son got on his horse and rode far away into another country. Far from his friends and his family, the boy figured that he could do whatever he wanted and that nobody he knew would know about it, so he spent all his money on fancy food and drinking and women and having parties. When he had finally wasted all his money, he had to go out and get a job, but the only thing he could find was a job feeding the pigs. Since he was so empty-handed, he lived on the leftover corn husks of the corn that he fed to the animals. Now, to the Jews, pigs were dirty animals, and they weren't allowed to eat pork or pig meat—or even be around them.

The younger son finally got mad at himself. He said, "I used to be rich in my fathers' house, but here I am feeding pigs, and eating their leftovers." So, he traveled back to his own country, and came to his father's house, crying. He said to his father, "I am so sorry, father. I wasted all the money, and I don't deserve to be treated as your son anymore. Please, can I just be one of your servants?

But the father was so glad to see his son that he thought he had lost forever, he ordered his servants to make a big feast for him. His older brother, however, when he heard what was happening, got mad. He complained to his father that "he always was there, doing whatever the father wanted, but his younger brother had run off and wasted all of his money on parties, and now he comes back, and he gets a big party. It's just not fair!"

The father hugged him and told that he was happy with the son who always was there, but he was very happy that the son he thought was lost and gone forever was saved. This was the meaning of the parables of the lost sheep, the lost coin, and the lost son. So God feels the same way when we go back to Him too.

About this time, the people of Galilee began to talk badly about Jesus. They were amazed about his miracles, but they wondered, "Isn't this the son of Joseph the Carpenter? We know the family; they aren't anyone special. We know all his brothers and sisters; they are just like us. How could this man come out of a common family like that?" When Jesus heard of these murmurings, he simply said, "A prophet can't be respected around his own family or his own town." It's a good lesson in life, that if you change to become a Godly person, your old friends and even your own family might not be able to accept it, because they knew what you were like before finding Christ in your heart. Jesus reasoned that he couldn't do what he now does to his own town, as its citizens had known him growing up.

It was also around this time that trouble was brewing. King Herod, the son of King Herod who had tried to have Jesus killed after he was born, was then the ruler over the Galilee region of Israel. He began to be worried about all the people who were following John the Baptist. King Herod had actually gone to some of John's teachings, and Herod respected John as a man of God, one who taught the Word of God well and with conviction.

20. Lazarus Lives Again

When He had said these things, He cried out with a loud voice, "Lazarus, come forth." The man who had died came forth, bound hand and foot with wrappings, and his face was wrapped around with a cloth. Jesus said to them, "Unbind him, and let him go."
(John 11:43-44)

Now, one day, Mary and Martha of Bethany, the same sisters who had had dinner with Jesus and who Mary had honored by washing his feet and anointing them with oil, found out that their brother Lazarus was dying. They thought that Jesus could do something about healing him, and they requested for him to heal their brother in Bethany. Jesus had become a friend of Lazarus before and came to heal him.

Jesus had other business to do, so it wasn't for two days that he could be able to leave to go to Bethany. His apostles warned him that people were after him in that area, and they wanted to stone him to death. But he loved Mary and Martha and Lazarus and told them that it was important for him to go to Bethany to help Lazarus.

Jesus told his apostles that Lazarus was sleeping, and they said—if he is resting let him rest. But then Jesus clarified himself, that God had shown him that Lazarus had died on his illness. Then the apostles understood him, and they still feared that Jesus would be captured and stoned to death himself, but they agreed that if Jesus was going to be stoned, they all wanted to go along and be stoned too.

When they got to Bethany, which was a long way away, they came near to the house of Mary and Martha. Mary was sad and stayed inside the house crying about her brother, but Martha ran out to meet Jesus on the road. She told him that Lazarus was dead, and if Jesus had arrived earlier, he could have saved him.

Now, by then, Lazarus had already been dead for four days. His body was wrapped in cloths and placed within a burial cave. In those days. bodies were not buried underground, but into special family caves. They had little shelves built into them, and bodies were placed onto a shelf, and a rock rolled over to cover the entrance of the cave.

Jesus told Martha that Lazarus would live once more. Martha replied, "Yes, Jesus, I know all about the resurrection, when all the dead will live again in heaven." Jesus corrected her, saying he wasn't talking about that resurrection, in the future. But that Lazarus would live again now. He told her:

> *"I am the resurrection and the life; he who believes in Me will live even if he dies, and everyone who lives and believes in Me will*

never die. Do you believe this?"
(John 11:25-26)

Martha said that totally believed Jesus was who he said he was and that God would do anything that Jesus asked for. She sent for Mary, who was still in her house mourning. When she heard that Jesus was on the road outside of Bethany, she ran out of the house, leaving friends behind, to run to Jesus. All her friends followed her, and they were all crying about Lazarus too.

Mary cried out to Jesus, hugging him, and asking him why it took so long. She was a little mad at Jesus, thinking that he would have healed him if he had gotten there quicker. Then even Jesus cried in Mary's arms about his lost friend Lazarus. They went to the burial cave, and Jesus ordered some of the men in the crowd to roll away the stone that blocked it. It smelled really bad there because Lazarus had been deceased 4 days ago. Jesus ignored the smell and then prayed to God out loud:

"Father, I thank You that You have heard Me. I knew that You always hear Me; but because of the people standing around I said it, so that they may believe that You sent Me."

(John 11:41-42)

Jesus cried in a loud voice, "Lazarus, come out!" And then soon, Lazarus appeared from the cave, still wrapped in the burial cloths around his body, and a burial napkin on his face. They helped unwrap Lazarus and dress him in normal clothes.

Many people came to Mary and Martha's house, to hear the wonderful story of how Jesus had raised their brother Lazarus from the grave. But when word got to the chief priests in the Temple, they began to plot Jesus' death. They were scared of anyone who could raise a dead man because they knew they didn't have that sort of power.

21. Bartimaeus Receives His Sight

And answering him, Jesus said, "What do you want Me to do for you?" And the blind man said to Him, "Rabboni, I want to regain my sight!" And Jesus said to him, "Go; your faith has made you well." Immediately he regained his sight and began following Him on the road.
(Mark 10:51-52)

J esus and his apostles traveled across the Jordan River again, preaching in the Jewish villages on that side of the river, and Jesus began to warn his apostles that there would be a day soon that the government would capture him, torture him, and kill him—but he told them not to be upset, as he promised his resurrection on the third day.

It scared the apostles, and they all swore to him that they would protect him against all those things, even if it meant that had to lay down their lives for Jesus. But Jesus assured them all that it was all written about in the old prophecies of the prophets and confirmed to him by the spirits of Moses and Elisha on the Mount of Transfiguration. They were all concerned about Jesus, but he assured them that he had to be sacrificed to pay for the sins of the whole world.

Now, they crossed over the river again and went along the road from Jericho towards Jerusalem. There, they came across a blind man on the ground, begging for pennies so that he could eat. The name was named Bartimaeus, and he had heard all about all the miracles that Jesus had performed. As Jesus went by, the blind man uttered, "Jesus, son of David, have mercy on me!"

Jesus stopped and called to people in the crowd to bring the blind man to him. They went over to where he was sitting, and helped him up, and led him to Jesus. Jesus looked at him and asked, "What do you want me to do for you?"

The blind man replied, "Lord, that I may receive my sight."

Seeing that the blind man really believed that Jesus was the son of God and that God could do anything that Jesus asked of Him, Jesus said, "Go your way, because your believing has healed you." And immediately the blind man could see.

22. The Conversion of Zaccheus

And Jesus said to him, "Today salvation has come to this house, because he, too, is a son of Abraham. For the Son of Man has come to seek and to save that which was lost."
(Luke 19:9-10)

After Jesus healed the blind man, the group passed by Jericho—and many people lined the road, just for the chance to see Jesus and the apostles pass by. One person in the crowd was a rich tax collector. He was not Jewish and generally hated by the people he had to collect taxes to give to the Romans. However, he had heard about Jesus and wanted to see him for himself.

Unfortunately, when the man whose name was

Zacchaeus got to the road, he couldn't see anything. He was very short, and there were so many people lining the road like a parade that he couldn't see over them. So, he got an idea—he climbed up into a sycamore tree that was close to the road, and from up there he could see above the crowd. Eventually, everyone got excited because they could see Jesus, and the apostles, and a large crowd following them up the road from Jericho.

When Jesus got up to precisely where the sycamore tree was, he stopped suddenly and looked up directly at Zacchaeus. Jesus said, "Zacchaeus, get down out of that tree, and come to me. I am going to spend the night at your house."

All the people watching got a little mad because they knew Zacchaeus was the local tax collector, and they didn't like him at all. Why had Jesus decided to spend the night in his house, they asked?

Jesus and the apostles went with Zacchaeus to his house, and Jesus asked him what sort of man he was. He told Jesus that he was an honest tax collector, he didn't intentionally harm or overcharge anyone, and if he did accidentally, he paid the man back out of his own pocket four times what he had wrongly taken.

Jesus determined that the man would become blessed because even though he wasn't Jewish, he believed in Jesus and he was a descendant of Abraham. His honesty and faith in God would save his whole family from hell. It was a foreshadow of what would happen soon, that even though the Jews were God's chosen people, he loved all the Gentiles as well if they would believe in Him.

Now, after leaving the house of Zacchaeus, the group walked north to the town of Bethany and came to the house of Mary and Martha. Lazarus was there too. Once again, Mary washed Jesus' feet with oil and dried it with her hair. This time, however, Judas was there, and he objected, saying that this oil cost a lot of money—isn't it better to sell it and donate it to the poor, rather than using it to clean Jesus' feet? Jesus replied, "Leave her alone; she is doing this in preparation for my burial. You'll always have poor people, but I won't be around much longer."

23. Jesus Enters Jerusalem

The crowds going ahead of Him, and those who
followed, were shouting,
"Hosanna to the Son of David; Blessed is He
Who Comes in the Name of the Lord.
Hosanna in the highest!"
When He had entered Jerusalem, all the city
was stirred, saying, "Who is this?" And the
crowds were saying, "This is the prophet, Jesus,
from Nazareth in Galilee."
(Matthew 21:9-11)

After the evening with Martha and her siblings, Jesus and the apostles went west towards Jerusalem. When they got to the little village of Bethpage, Jesus told his apostles to go into the village and borrow a donkey—specifically one that has a young baby colt. Jesus knew of an ancient prophet who had written of this moment, who wrote that the King would enter Jerusalem on a donkey, with His son riding on it.

The right donkey was found and brought to Jesus, and they put robes on it for Jesus to ride upon. The crowd that followed him got ahead of him, and laid their clothes onto the road, and cut palm branches down for the trees near the road. This was an event that was prophesied by the prophet Zechariah hundreds of years before, who wrote that "Rejoice greatly, O daughter of Zion; shout O daughter of Jerusalem; behold, the King comes to you; he is just, and has salvation; lowly, riding upon a donkey, and upon the donkey's baby."

Jesus rode towards Jerusalem with everyone cheering and chanting that the new King of Israel was coming into town. This was the event that is still celebrated today as Palm Sunday.

When he got close to it and could see the gates leading into it, he cried, talking about the future destruction of the city by the Romans, saying if you only knew what your future held! The city will be destroyed, not one stone of this Temple will be left on another because you have rejected me.

The next morning, Jesus and his followed entered Jerusalem, and Jesus was hungry. He saw a fig tree in someone's yard, and couldn't find any figs on it. Fig trees at the time were considered the "people's fruit", and it was acceptable for a stranger to take a fig off the tree to eat. But this one only had leaves, not figs. Jesus looked at the tree and said, "No fruit will ever grow on this tree." Jesus was actually talking about the Jews in the city, who had failed to believe when the Messiah was there and that they too were soon going to wither away. This is exactly what happened. In the year 70 AD, the Romans destroyed Jerusalem, wrecked the Temple so not one stone sat on another one, then scattered the Jews all over the Roman Empire, and it wasn't until 1948 that Israel became a country again.

24. Trouble in the Temple

And Jesus entered the temple and drove out all those who were buying and selling in the temple, and overturned the tables of the money changers and the seats of those who were selling doves.
(Matthew 21:12)

J esus went straight towards the Temple that King Herod had built and came into the street leading towards its entrance. There were booths that had been set up by people who could change the Jewish money into Persian coins because the Jewish money was nearly worthless, and the Persian money had become the only coins that the priests of the Temple have decided to accept for donations. Because of having to change from one coin to the other, the Jewish people lost money every time they came to the Temple to worship, while the moneychangers and the priests got rich.

There were also people in the booths selling animals for the sacrifices. These were sickly lambs and doves, that the merchants bought for a few pennies, and sold to the worshippers for a lot more. Why not? they thought, they were only going to be killed soon afterward anyway. There was also a constant haggling going on between the moneychangers and the sellers of sacrificial animals with their customers, that nobody could hear the services in the Temple.

When Jesus entered the street, God showed him that every one of the merchants there were only thinking of their own greed. None of them were honestly selling anything that pleased God. Jesus became enraged for once in his life, with a rage that God felt towards them, and knocked over the tables and cursed at the men, calling them evil and that they don't deserve to be doing anything in God's Temple.

Jesus cried out "My house is supposed to be an example of God to all the people in the world, but you have turned it into a den of thieves."

Children were still calling out "Hosanna, the King of the Jews." The chief priests of the Temple were angered by Jesus coming in like he owned the place and that the children were calling out to worship him. They went to Jesus, and asked, "Do you hear what the children are saying?" Jesus looked at the priests and said, "Out of the mouths of babes and suckling, there is perfect praise."

After leaving the Temple, Jesus and the apostles returned to Bethany. The next morning, they passed by the fig tree again and saw that it had completely withered away.

When they got to the Temple, the priests there tried to accuse him of blaspheming God, a crime there punishable by death. This was an attempt by the priests to get evidence on him to charge him with this crime. It failed, but before the priests left Jesus told them four parables about them. Two of the parables were about a vineyard, and two about a marriage feast, so they could see what their conduct looked to Jesus and to God. Instead of being faithful workers for God, they were behaving as self-serving, wicked servants and false prophets.

After leaving the Temple, Jesus met with his apostles on the Mount of Olives. There they questioned him about the end times. Throughout his ministry, everyone around him had expected his to be a conquering king, to rid them of the Roman government controlling Israel, and establish his own kingdom. It was finally becoming apparent to all of them that it was not the time for that to happen.

They asked, "Tell us, when will you come back to set up your kingdom, and what will be the signs of your second coming?"

Jesus told them, "Nobody knows the hour, except for my Father. There will be wars and rumors of wars, and the days will become like the days of Noah when everyone does what he feels like doing without any obedience to God or His word. But watch like a watchman, and you'll know when the days are close."

He also told them about the Rapture of the believers from the world. He said there will be a day when two people are working in the field—one is taken, and the other is left behind. And two women working together milling grain, when one is taken and the other is left. This Rapture will happen to remove all of God's children off of the world—before the devil gets his final chance to ruin it

Then, Jesus told his apostles about several parables to help them understand more clearly. One was about ten unmarried women. They went out to meet their future husbands, carrying lamps. But five of the women were foolish and didn't put oil into their lamps. The other five were wise and filled their lamps before they went out. The foolish women were locked out of the room because they were not properly prepared. God wants us to always be ready for Christ to come back for us.

The second parable was about a rich man and his servants. The rich man gave coins to three of his servants, according to how well he trusted them. To one he gave five coins, to another two coins, and to the third one coin. Then the rich man went on a trip. The servant with the five coins used them to trade for other items, and when the rich man returned, the servant had doubled his money. The servant with the two coins also doubled the man's money and was praised. The man who only had one coin had buried it, and could only give the man back the same coin he had been given. The rich man took his coin away and gave it to another. Jesus said the lesson of this parable is that God came into the world to give mankind an opportunity to prosper—but if you are lazy and disobedient and fail to believe in God, in the end, you may end up losing everything.

25. The Last Supper

While they were eating, Jesus took some bread, and after a blessing, He broke it and gave it to the disciples, and said, "Take, eat; this is My body." And when He had taken a cup and given thanks, He gave it to them, saying, "Drink from it, all of you; for this is My blood of the covenant, which is poured out for many for the forgiveness of sins."
(Matthew 26:26-28)

Now, Jesus met with his apostles to share their last meal together at Martha's house in Bethany, on the Sabbath before the Passover holiday. It would begin the last week of Jesus' life on earth. All twelve of the apostles were with him.

A typical meal in Israel at the time consisted of a sort of a stew, with whatever meat they could afford, and a mixture of vegetables, cooked over an open fire. Everyone would sit on the floor, around a low table that was only maybe six inches off the floor. Their bread was not like modern bread, but a flatbread like what we now call pita bread. Spoons had not yet been invented, so this stew was poured into bowls, and then pieces of the pita-type bread would be broken off and used to dip into the stew to get the food.

Jesus was teaching them that every time they ate a meal, they should remember him, and how he was soon going to give his own body to be broken to pay for all the illnesses that a man can have. So, he took his bread, and tore it into small pieces, and handed each of his friends a piece. He prayed thanks to God, and He told them, take this and eat it, and you will remember my body which will become broken for you.

Then he took his wine glass, it may have been a glass or even a clay cup because both were common at the time. He took his cup, prayed for that too, and told his men to take their cups of wine and take a sip, to remember that I must shed my blood for the removal of sins too.

Throughout the Old Testament, people have sacrificed animals as a payment for sin. The earliest recorded was when God told Abraham to take his only son Isaac up into a mountain to sacrifice for Him. Abraham assumed that it meant he had to sacrifice Isaac to God, but God supplied a lamb instead. During the first Passover, Moses told the Israelites to sacrifice young lambs and sprinkle its blood on the doors so the angel of Death would go over their houses. Throughout all the years of the Temple, the priests sacrificed lambs or small pigeons.

His men didn't fully understand what he meant by all these things, because they hadn't been told exactly all what was going to happen, but they remembered what he told them afterward, and the practice of the holy communion is still practiced in the church today. But the deeper meaning that Jesus was teaching was to remember his sacrifice at every meal you have, breakfast, lunch, and dinner, and always be thankful that God can forgive your sins if you ask Him.

During the meal, Jesus and Judas Iscariot both reached into the pot at the same time, and Jesus said that Judas was going to betray him. Judas had already gone to the chief priests in the Temple and told them that he would betray Christ for thirty silver coins. Jesus didn't know that, but God told him.

After they had eaten, Jesus poured a bowl full of water and washed each of the apostle's feet. This was a symbol of service to them. Peter objected, saying that the Master should not be washing the servant's feet. But Jesus told him that it was a lesson to all of them, that God wants to us be servants to all mankind, and bless and teach everyone about God.

Then the apostles and friends sat around him as Jesus began a long teaching just for their ears. In it, he told them some wonderful things about God. He said that he was preparing a place for all of them in heaven, and someday they would see the wonderful mansions for them to live in forever. He said that they had all seen God because Jesus did all the works of the Father during his ministry on earth. And he told them there would come a day soon that the Holy Spirit would come to all of them, and they could do the same sorts of miracles that they had seen Jesus do, and even great things because Jesus was returning to God. He said that this Holy Spirit would be a great comforter to them, to whisper the words of God to them.

Finally, at the end of the teaching, Jesus prayed for them a wonderful prayer. He thanked God for their lives and all they had been through together. He prayed that they would remember his words, and spread them out into the entire world after he was gone. He prayed that they would live their lives close to the heart of God—like Jesus had lived his life—and be forever blessed to serve God. Some of the most memorable words Jesus spoke were in this prayer, to his apostles but also to all of us today:

"Do not let your heart be troubled; do believe in God, and believe also in Me. In My Father's house are many dwelling places; if it were not so, I would have told you; for I go to prepare a place for you . . .. Believe Me, that I am in the Father and the Father is in Me; otherwise believe because of the works themselves. Truly, truly, I say to you, he who believes in Me, the works that I do, he will do also; and greater works than these he will do; because I go to the Father. Whatever you ask in My name, that will I do, so that the Father may be glorified in the Son. If you ask Me anything in My name, I will do it.... "If anyone loves Me, he will keep My word; and My Father will love him, and We will come to him and

make Our abode with him . . .. Peace I leave with you; My peace I give to you; not as the world gives do I give to you. Do not let your heart be troubled, nor let it be fearful. You heard that I said to you, 'I go away, and I will come to you.' If you loved Me, you would have rejoiced because I go to the is greater than I . . .. I am the true vine, and My Father is the vinedresser— for the Father. Every branch in Me that does not bear fruit, He takes away; and every branch that bears fruit, He prunes it so that it may bear more fruit. You are already clean because of the word which I have spoken to you. Abide in Me, and I in you. As the branch cannot bear the fruit of itself unless it abides in the vine, so neither can you unless you abide in Me. I am the vine, you are the branches; he who abides in Me and I in him, he bears much fruit, for apart from Me you can do nothing…. If anyone does not abide in Me, he is thrown away as a branch and dries up . . .. Just as the Father has loved Me, I have also loved you; abide in My love. If you keep My *commandments, you will abide in My love; just as I have kept My Father's commandments and abide in His love. These things I have spoken to you so that My joy may be in you, and that your joy may be made full. "This is My commandment, that you love one another, just as I have loved you. Greater love has no one than this, that one lay down his life for his friends.... This I command you, that you love one another. (**John 14:1,2; 11-14; 27-28, John 15:1-5; 9-13, 17**)*

Later that night, Jesus took his apostles from Martha's house in Bethany, over the Mount of Olives and down to the hill on the other side of the Temple, to a beautiful garden called Gethsemane. He told them to wait there for him, and they all sat down among the flowers, but Jesus told Peter, James, and John to follow him. Jesus was very sad and quiet as they walked farther up the hill. Then Jesus told them to wait and watch out for him, so they sat down also, while Jesus went still a little further.

Jesus got on his knees, and then laid all the way down with his arms stretched upon the ground as he prayed to God:

> *"My Father, if it is possible, let this cup pass from Me; yet not as I will, but as You will."*
> ### *(Matthew 26:39)*

Jesus knew from the scriptures of the prophets and from what God had told him that he was soon going to have to go through the most horrible torture and death that any man had ever gone through. Of course, he didn't what to have to go through it, but he believed that God would give him the strength he needed to get through it, and God's greater purpose for his life would soon make it all worthwhile. While he hoped for any other way to accomplish the goal of freeing mankind from all its sins, he accepted that if it was God's will that he went through it, he would.

His apostles had fallen asleep, so he woke them up and they all returned to Bethany and went to bed in Martha's house.

26. Mocked

And after twisting together a crown of thorns,
they put it on His head, and a reed in His right
hand; and they knelt down before Him and
mocked Him, saying, "Hail, King of the Jews!"
They spat on Him, and took the reed
and began to beat Him on the head.
(Matthew 27:29-30)

Judas, the betrayer, wasn't there but had left after dinner and met with the priests and had schemed with them that he would identify Christ to the soldiers that came to arrest him by giving Jesus a kiss on the cheek.

At midnight, Jesus awoke as Judas came marching down the road with the priests, and the elders of the city, and a large group of soldiers carrying swords and poles with metal arrowheads on them. When Judas got up to

Jesus, he kissed him on the cheek, and immediately the soldiers moved up to arrest Jesus. Peter pulled out his sword and cut off the ear of one of the soldiers arresting Jesus. But Jesus healed the soldier right on the spot and told his apostles that it was all going on as God had told him it would and that if he had really wanted to stop this from happening, God would send him thousands of angels if he asked for them.

So, the soldiers and the priests led Jesus away and took to a highly respected man named Annas, who said to send the prisoner to his son-in-law, the chief priest of the Temple, Caiaphas. Caiaphas asked him about what things Jesus taught, and Jesus told him that he had taught all about God and heaven and had always taught in the open. He said that everyone knew what he taught already, so why are you asking me this question—when you already know the answer?

One of the soldiers slapped Jesus across the face

for talking back to the High Priest, and they tied a blindfold over his eyes and hit him in the face and made fun of him. Caiaphas ordered that Jesus is brought before the council of Temple priests.

The Council chambers of the Sanhedrin, known as the Hall of Hewn Stone, was on the southwest corner of the Temple grounds. They were the most learned men of Jewish law and met together to make decisions about violations of Moses' laws. Now it was long after midnight, and the Sanhedrin had to all be woken up and come to the Hall under the cover of darkness.

They questioned Jesus, to try to find a legal way to have him executed. A number of people came by, to say that Jesus did this or that, but it was all according to God's laws. Finally, they brought in two witnesses, who said that Jesus had threatened to destroy the Temple in three days and that he was the Messiah, the Son of God. The Sanhedrin found Jesus guilty of treason and blasphemy against the church and said that he was worthy of death. But Caiaphas didn't want to be responsible to kill him directly, so he sent Jesus to the Roman governor of Judea.

The Judgment Hall in Jerusalem was the palace of the Roman Governor. It had a large mosaic floor from out the Hall, which is mentioned in the Bible. It was early in the morning, with the sun just coming up. Because it was the morning of the Passover holiday, which would begin at sundown, the members of the Sanhedrin would not go inside the palace but asked the governor to come out to them. The Roman governor was a man named Pontius Pilate. Pilate asked what charges they had against this Jesus. They replied that Jesus was a criminal, the Sanhedrin wasn't allowed to execute anyone, only the governor could sentence him to death.

Pilate took Jesus into the Judgment Hall, and questioned him, "Are you the King of the Jews?" Jesus replied that he was a king, but not of the current world and time. Pilate decided there was no reason to execute him, and went out to tell that to the Sanhedrin outside. The Jews were upset, but when Pilate heard that Jesus had mostly taught in the Galilee, he decided to send his to the overseer of that region, King Herod.

Herod was glad to see Jesus, having heard many wonderful things about him, and hope to see Jesus perform some miracles for him. But Jesus just stood there silently, making Herod mad. He sent Jesus back to Pilate.

It was a tradition then that he would release one prisoner out of two, just before the Passover, and let the Jews decide which one to let go. Pilate wanted to let Jesus go free, but he was bound by rules not to allow that. So, he got a vicious murderer out of jail, named Barabbas, and offered to the crowd which had formed to let one go, and to kill the other one. He figured that Barabbas was so very bad, there was no way the people would choose him to be freed. In the back of the crowd, the priests began to chant, "Kill Jesus, kill Jesus", and soon the entire crowd was chanting it too. So, Governor Pilate went over to a bowl of water and washed his hands and told the crowd that his blood would be on them. He would do as they asked and kill Jesus and let Barabbas go free.

Then the soldiers of Pilate took Jesus into a large hall in the governor's house, and stripped off his clothes, and put one of the governor's scarlet colored royal robes on him. One man ran outside and got a piece of a bush with long, strong thorns on it, and they put it around his head like a crown and twisted the ends together until the thorns cut deeply into his head, and blood began to drip down his hair and face. But Jesus just stood silently and proudly.

Then they found a thick stick and placed it in his hand, and the soldiers bowed down in front of him, making fun of him, saying "Hail, King of the Jews." They all took turns spitting into his face, and hitting him all over with the stick, and punching him in the face. Then the soldiers took a whip, with long leather strips that had broken bones or glass or sharp metal tied on the ends, and beat Jesus with it. The sharp ends would cut into his skin and rip big chunks out of his back and stomach and arms and legs. It was terribly painful, but Jesus just stood there and never said a word. Soon Jesus was bloody and bruised all over, with big bruises on his eyes and nose and mouth, so that he hardly even looked human now.

Pilate brought the bloody Jesus out again before the Priests, hoping that they would have compassion on the man. They just said, "Crucify him, crucify him." Pilate led Jesus out again before all the people, and told them "Behold your king!" They answered, "We have no king but Caesar, crucify him!" So Pilate was forced to order it, and they led Jesus away to be executed.

Jesus stood tall and proud for all the abuse. He

knew must go through all the torture, worse than any man ever had, to pay the price for every time anyone is abused, or called bad names, or made fun of, or beaten in life. Jesus went through it all, so we can all stand proud too when all the evils of the world try to beat us down. Because Jesus went through it all for us, we can stand proud through anything too, knowing God is with us.

27. The Crucifixion and Death of Jesus

*And when they came to a place called Golgotha,
which means Place of a Skull, they gave
Him wine to drink mixed with gall; and after
tasting it, He was unwilling to drink. And when
they had crucified Him, they divided up His
garments among themselves by
casting lots... And Jesus cried out again with a
loud voice and yielded up His spirit.*
(Matthew 27:33-35, 50)

Now, after the soldiers had mocked Jesus, they put his real clothes back on him and led him away to be crucified. It's not used anymore, but crucifixion was a way the Romans used to kill their slaves who had committed serious crimes. It was to be a warning to other slaves to be obedient to their masters. A large tree was firmly planted onto the ground, and then a prisoner had his hands nailed to a board, with his arms stretched high and wide. Above that board was another, with the crime they committed written on it. The prisoners were usually forced to walk from the prison to the place of hanging with the board nailed through their hands so that everyone could see them being led to their death. The board was then nailed to the tree, thus making a cross. The prisoner would hang on the board until he died from starvation or being strangled.

Two other criminals were also led from the prison towards the execution place. Jesus was too badly beaten to walk with the board, so the soldiers grabbed a man from the crowd, who was there to celebrate the Passover, and made him carry the board through the streets of Jerusalem, His name of Simon, a Cyrenian.

The soldier's led Jesus up to the place on the east

side of the Jordan River, across from the Temple, at a place called the Place of the Skull. There is still a rock formation there that does look just like a skull. They took some water mixed with something that was supposed to help the prisoner not feel as much pain while he was dying, but Jesus tasted it and spit it out and refused to take any more of it. He had to go through the entire thing without a sedative.

So, they removed his outer clothes, leaving him in only his underwear, and nailed the board to the tree. A large crowd gathered to watch it happen, including his own mother, Mary. The solder's nailed other criminals to the trees around Jesus, too.

Since it was Passover, ready to start in just a few hours, many thousands of people had come to the Temple to worship God. From the Temple, you can see across the Kidron Valley to the Place of the Skull, where Jesus was hanging. Jesus was quiet and peaceful, while everyone else around him was crying. His own mother, Mary, was there shaking and crying, as were many other of his friends and family.

The priests took another board, and wrote on it: "Jesus of Nazareth, King of the Jews" and had it nailed above his head. The soldiers laughed at Jesus too, saying things like, "If you are really the King, call on God to get you off the cross!"

As Jesus hung on the cross, one of the others who was sacrificed with him asked him "Can you save me too?" Jesus told him, yes, I promise you today, that I will see you in paradise." The others hanging there laughed at him, but Jesus was promising that when the earth became a paradise again, at his first Coming, that man would be raised from the dead and have eternal life.

Suddenly, the skies grew dark with thick clouds, and it was like night time from about 3 o'clock to 6 o'clock. After the clouds moved away, the priests began to tell the soldiers that they had to kill Jesus because it was getting close to nighttime, and they couldn't allow him to hang there once the Passover meal was started. One of the soldiers took a spear with a long metal arrowhead on it and shoved it into his belly just below his ribs, far up to pierce his internal organs. Jesus began to bleed heavily from the wound.

As he stood there exhausted, he cried to God, "My God, my God, for Your purpose I have given my life." A few minutes later, Jesus died on the cross.

Right after he died, Jerusalem was hit by a strong earthquake, and the crowd watching the crucifixion and all the worshippers in the Temple fell onto the ground. Inside the Temple, a thick curtain that covered the Holy of Holies was torn in half from the top to the bottom. Many people there said, "Truly, this was the Son of God that was just killed."

Jesus died at the beginning of the Passover, as the perfect Passover sacrifice, the perfect Lamb, the perfect Adam, who was wounded to pay for all the sins of mankind. Beaten and bruised, mocked and spit on, Jesus endured everything a man could ever go through, so he would be the perfect payment in full for all the sins of mankind since Adam first sinned. Jesus was the perfect Passover lamb, paying for sin not just for one year, but for all time. Now, we can go to Jesus when we sin, and ask him to forgive us of those sins too. And in the future, Jesus can lead us to heaven as spotless and pure, to enter into paradise forever.

28. Jesus Is Risen

The angel said to the women, "Do not be afraid;
for I know that you are looking for Jesus who
has been crucified. He is not here, for He has
risen, just as He said. Come, see the place where
He was lying. Go quickly and tell His disciples
that He has risen from the dead; and behold, He
is going ahead of you into Galilee, there you will
see Him; behold, I have told you."
(Matthew 28:5-7)

A rich man named Joseph of Arimathea, who had a burial cave nearby, and one of Jesus's disciples, went to Mary, Jesus' mother, and told the family that Jesus could be laid to rest in his burial cave. His burial cave was nearby, and it had been freshly dugout and didn't have any other bodies in it. They agreed, and Joseph had the body taken down off the cross and wrapped in a clean white linen cloth and placed into Joseph's wagon. The family followed the wagon to the burial cave, and the body was placed inside on one of the burial niches. Mary and the others went to Jerusalem to buy spices and oil to prepare the body and soon returned to put them on the it. When they were done, a large stone was rolled over in front of the cave to seal it off. The crowd cried as the burial was happening, including Mary Magdalene and Mary, the mother of Jesus.

The next day, the Jewish priests came to Pontius Pilate and asked that he guard the grave, fearing that someone might steal the body and hide it, and they might try to say that Jesus had risen from the dead. Pilate ordered his soldiers to seal up the stone at the burial cave, so it couldn't be opened and set guards there to make sure nobody came close.

A few days later, on Sunday morning, Mary

Magdalene and Mary, the mother of Jesus, walked down to the grave cave. There was another earthquake, and an angel appeared, and the stone rolled away from the cave. The soldiers guarding the cave passed out cold from the sight of the angel. When the women got there, the angel said to them, "Jesus isn't here, he has risen from the dead. Go look inside the cave for yourself."

They went into the cave and saw the linen burial cloth and the cloth they had laid over his face, just lying on the shelf with nobody inside it. They came out and the angel said, "Go back to Galilee, that's where you will see the risen Christ."

Mary turned around and saw a man standing there that she assumed was a gardener because she didn't recognize him. She asked if he had seen anyone come and steal the body of Jesus out of the cave. The man just said, "Mary" and she immediately recognized the voice, and knew it was Jesus, risen from the dead. She wanted to run over and give him a big hug, but he told her not to touch him, as he first had to go to heaven and present himself to God.

29. Doubting Thomas

But Thomas, one of the twelve, called Didymus, was not with them when Jesus came. So the other disciples were saying to him, "We have seen the Lord!" But he said to them, "Unless I see in His hands the imprint of the nails, and put my finger into the place of the nails, and put my hand into His side, I will not believe."

(John 20:24-25)

Now, when Mary went back to the apostles, she found them all hiding in the upper room of an inn. They were all afraid that the priests would be coming after them, too. She told the apostles that they had seen the angel of God, about seeing Jesus, about the Angel, about the empty tomb, and about the fact that they were all supposed to go back to Galilee and that there they would all see the risen Jesus Christ. However, the apostles still couldn't believe the things that Mary said were really true.

The next day, two of Christ's disciples were walking from Jerusalem to a small village nearby called Emmaus. As they cried and talked about the horrible execution of Jesus, another man came up behind them and asked why they were so sad. They said, "Are you a stranger here, didn't you see what happened in Jerusalem a few days ago?" The stranger asked, "What things." The men told the stranger all about Jesus, and his ministry, and his miracles, and what horrible things were done to him, and the things that Mary had told them about the empty tomb and seeing the risen Christ.

Then, as they walked along, the stranger told the two all about the ancient prophecies that had been written about the Messiah, and they thought he was a wise man, and invited him to come to their house and have dinner. He agreed, and as they broke bread together, their eyes were opened and they realized that this was the risen Christ they had been talking to. And then Jesus vanished out of their sight.

The next day, as the apostles were still gathered together in the upper room of the inn, Jesus appeared to all of them himself. He said, "Peace be unto you," and he showed them the wounds on his hands where they were nailed to the cross, and the wound on his stomach that had been pierced by a spear, they were all amazed and happy to see him.

Jesus asked, "Do you have anything to eat?" They gave him a piece of a broiled fish, and a section of sweet honeycomb, dripping with honey. Then he taught them that very soon they would be able to receive the Holy Spirit into themselves, and when they saw the tongues like fire, they were to breathe in deeply.

After Jesus left, one of the apostles, Thomas,

showed up. He wasn't there to see Jesus, told everyone else that he didn't believe it. He said, "I can only believe it if I can see it for myself, with my own eyes."

Eight days later, they were still all locked into the room waiting to return to Galilee. Jesus appeared to them again and focused his attention this time on Thomas. He told him to look at his hands, so see the holes left by the nails and to stick a finger into the holes. And Jesus said to reach into his stomach, to see for yourself that it is the actual wound from the cross.

Thomas did as Jesus said, and was finally convinced that this could only be the risen Christ. He told Jesus, "My Lord and my God."

Jesus looked at him, and making sure that everyone could hear him, Jesus said, "Thomas, because you saw me, you believed. Blessed is everyone who can't actually see me, but still believe in me." He was talking about you and me because we can't see Christ, but we can still believe!

After they saw Jesus in Jerusalem, they all returned to their own homes in Galilee. Jesus continued to appear to them, to teach them things they needed to know. On one occasion, Peter and Thomas and other apostles and disciples were together on the Sea of Tiberius, the Roman name for the Lake Kinnereth. They were all together to go fishing all night but didn't happen to catch anything.

The next morning, Jesus appeared to them all by the seashore, and called out "Do you have anything to eat?"

They answered no, and Jesus told them to throw out their fishing net. They did, and when they pulled it back out of the water, it was full of fish. They came back to shore, and started a fire, and had a wonderful breakfast together of bread and fried fish.

Those scriptures give us a clue what living will be like in our own future. We will have wonderful eternal bodies like Jesus now has. We will be able to be with our friends and family. We will still eat and be able to enjoy each other's company. We won't be floating around in the clouds, but walking on the earth enjoying it as it is turned back into Paradise.

30. The Ascension

And after He had said these things, He was lifted while they were looking on, and a cloud received Him out of their sight. And as they were gazing intently into the sky while He was going, behold, two men in white clothing stood beside them. They also said, "Men of Galilee, why do you stand looking into the sky? This Jesus, who has been taken up from you into heaven, will come in just the same way as you have watched Him go into heaven."

(Acts 1:9-11)

For a total of forty days, Jesus appeared to the apostles in Galilee and taught them those things they had to know to carry on his mission on earth. He also appeared before Peter and James—and at least once in front of a crowd of five hundred of his followers

Finally, Jesus knew it was time for him to leave the earth. He told the apostles to go back down to Jerusalem and meet them on top of the Mount of Olives.

When Jesus appeared before them on the Mount of Olives, on a fortieth day after the crucifixion. Jesus told them that it was time for him to leave. All the apostles were there, except Judas. Jesus told them that they all had a special mission:

"You will receive power when the Holy Spirit has come upon you, and you shall be My witnesses both in Jerusalem, and in all Judea and Samaria, and even to the remotest part of the earth."
(Acts 1:8)

"Go therefore and make disciples of all the nations, baptizing them in the name of the Father and the Son and the Holy Spirit, teaching them to observe all that I commanded you; and lo, I am with you always, even to the

*end of the age." (**Matthew 28:19-20**)*

After Jesus had taught them all about the Holy Spirit to come to them, he promised them, "I am with you always, until the end of the world." Then he told them to walk with him down the mountain on the road towards Bethany.

As they walked, the apostles asked him, "When are you coming back to conquer the Romans and take over as the eternal King?" Jesus told them all that the time was a secret, and nobody knew the hour but God. But until then, they were all to go back to Jerusalem and wait for the sign of the Holy Spirit, to receive the Holy Spirit and teach the whole world about him. They were, "to be witnesses of him to Judea, and in Samaria, and unto the uttermost parts of the earth." Even then, the apostles didn't realize that he meant to teach not only the Jews—but to everyone else, too.

When he was done saying these things to them,

Jesus was lifted into the clouds and disappeared. The men all stared upwards at the cloud in amazement, but they looked and found that two men were standing there in pure white robes. They knew they were angels.

The angels told them, "Why are you staring up into the sky? This same Jesus will return one day in the same way."

So, the apostles returned off the Mount of Olives to Bethany and then went to the room that they had rented in Jerusalem and waited for the sign of the Holy Spirit from God that Jesus had promised to them.

This completed Christ's personal ministry on the earth. Although the four gospels contain many wonderful things about him, it was written that there were so many other things that he did that weren't written down that the world couldn't even hold all the books that could be written about it. But the gospels were sufficient for people to know that Jesus was the Christ, the Son of God and that anyone can have eternal life by believing in his name.

31. The Holy Spirit

When the day of Pentecost had come, they were all together in one place. And suddenly there came from heaven a noise like a violent rushing wind, and it filled the whole house where they were sitting. And there appeared to them tongues as of fire distributing themselves, and they rested on each one of them. And they were all filled with the Holy Spirit and began to speak with other tongues, as the Spirit was giving them utterance.

(Acts 2:1-4)

N ow, the next week was a special one called Pentecost. It was another one of those Jewish holidays when everyone was supposed to come to Jerusalem and worship at the large Temple there. It was celebrated fifty days after Passover, called

Pentecost, or the Feast of the First Fruits, because it celebrated the first of the crops being ready to eat. Since Jesus was the Passover lamb for all eternity, they would celebrate the First Fruits of the Holy Spirit on that day.

The apostles rented the same room that they had before in Jerusalem, in the upper floor of an inn, where Jesus had previously shown himself before them, and to Mary, and to the doubting Thomas. Mary came there to visit them, and they had meals together and discussed Jesus and all they had seen and heard.

While the apostles were at Jerusalem, they decided that they had to appoint a new disciple to fill Judas's place among the twelve leaders of the group. Judas had killed himself because he was so sad about having betrayed Jesus. Judas had taken a sword, and stuck it into the ground, and fell on it so that his insides came out. The priests had him buried in the same poor peoples' cemetery that the priests had bought with the 30 pieces of silver they had bribed Judas with.

The apostles called a meeting of the disciples, who numbered about 120 people, and picked out two of the strongest believers they knew, Joseph and Matthias. The crowd voted, and they picked Matthias to become the replacement for Judas.

The city of Jerusalem was very crowded with people who came for the Pentecost celebration, and there was hardly any room to move about the outer courts of the Temple. On the day of the Pentecost celebration, the apostles all went to the Temple together, to worship according to Jewish law. They found an open spot and seated down in a circle. Suddenly there came a sound like a rushing mighty wind, and the apostles looked up and saw what looked like a ball of fire coming down from heaven. As it neared them, twelve tongues came out and stood above each one of their heads.

They knew this was the sign from God that Jesus

had told them about. They all took a deep breath and began to speak in other tongues. Some were earthly languages; some were speaking the language of the angels. The languages kept changing, and all the people around them heard the twelve apostles praising God in their own language.

There were Parthians, Medes, Persians, Egyptians, Libyans, Crete, Arabians, and many others—and they all heard the men speaking in their own language. Many were amazed to hear these men of Galilee praising God in their own language, speaking the wonderful works of God. It was amazing!

The visitors all around the apostles stood dumbfounded, with their mouths open. Some people just cried out that they were drunk. When Peter stood up and cried out "Men of Jerusalem, and Judea, and around the world, don't be shocked. We aren't drunk, it's only noon. No, no, this is what was prophesied hundreds of years ago by the Prophet Joel, that God would pour out His Holy Spirit unto anyone who believes in Jesus Christ, the risen savior of man.!"

32. New Recruits

*And with many other words, he
solemnly testified and kept on exhorting them,
saying, "Be saved from this perverse
generation!" So then, those who had received his
word were baptized; and that day there were
added about three thousand souls. They
were continually devoting themselves to the
apostles' teaching and to fellowship, to the
breaking of bread and to prayer.*
(Acts 2:40-42)

O n the day of Pentecost, Peter went on to teach everyone about Jesus Christ and his ministry on earth, of salvation, shaking a fist at the ones in the crowd who had called for Jesus's death. He taught everyone that God had raised Jesus from the dead, that he is now Lord of the Universe and the Christ and the

Messiah that everyone had looked forward to for millennia.

Peter told them that King David had also prophesied about Jesus. David had written that he believed in the Messiah and that he knew he would die someday but that a Messiah would be born and David would be raised from the dead to live with the promised Christ. And this Jesus, who was recently killed, was that risen savior and is both Lord and Christ.

"Men of Israel, listen to these words: Jesus the Nazarene, a man attested to you by God with miracles and wonders and signs which God performed through Him in your midst, just as you yourselves know— this Man, delivered over by the predetermined plan and foreknowledge of God, you nailed to a cross by the hands of godless men and put Him to death. But God raised Him up again, putting an end to the agony of death since it was impossible for Him to be held in its power. For

David says of Him,

'I SAW THE LORD ALWAYS IN MY PRESENCE;

HE IS AT MY RIGHT HAND SO THAT I WILL NOT BE

SHAKEN.

'THEREFORE MY HEART WAS GLAD AND MY TONGUE

EXULTED;

MOREOVER, MY FLESH ALSO WILL LIVE IN HOPE;

BECAUSE YOU WILL NOT ABANDON MY SOUL

TO HADES,

NOR ALLOW YOUR HOLY ONE TO UNDERGO DECAY.

'YOU HAVE MADE KNOWN TO ME THE WAYS OF LIFE;

YOU WILL MAKE ME FULL OF GLADNESS WITH YOUR

PRESENCE.'

Brethren, I may confidently say to you
regarding the patriarch David that he both died
and was buried, and his tomb is with us to this
day. And so, because he was a prophet and
knew that GOD HAD SWORN TO HIM WITH AN OATH
TO SEAT one OF HIS DESCENDANTS ON HIS
THRONE, he looked ahead and spoke of the
resurrection of the Christ, that HE WAS NEITHER

*ABANDONED TO HADES, NOR DID His flesh SUFFER DECAY. This Jesus God raised up again, to which we are all witnesses. Therefore, having been exalted to the right hand of God, and having received from the Father the promise of the Holy Spirit, He has poured forth this which you both see and hear. (**Acts 2:22-33**)*

Three thousand men and women in the audience believed the words of Peter, and the church began on that day. The apostles divided everyone into groups, and with the other elder disciples who had personally been with Jesus, began to meet in smaller groups to share meals together and to tell the new believers all about the things Jesus had taught them during his ministry, and all the wonderful things they had personally witnessed.

They continued to grow, passing the message of Christ from one house to the next, sharing meals, teaching, and singing praises to God. Many even gave everything they had to the needs of the growing church, so food and clothing and such could be bought for the new believers who needed anything. As the apostles went out, the message of Jesus Christ was passed throughout all the land of Judea, into the cities of Galilee and Samaria, and into the countries that surrounded them.

One day, Peter and John went to the Temple to worship, and they encountered a lame man sitting near the Beautiful Gate. There was a high wall around Jerusalem, with twelve gates around it, each with a different name. The man was sitting there, begging for food, and the apostles saw him and taught him about God and Jesus and told him, "In the name of Jesus Christ of Nazareth, rise up and walk."

They helped the man up, and as he rose, his legs were healed. He ran into the Temple, leaping, and praising God. He hugged Peter and John, and the people around them were amazed. Peter began to preach to the crowd, "Why are you all so amazed? The God of Abraham and Isaac can do anything and healed him. And Jesus, who YOU crucified, an innocent man, died to pay for all YOUR sins. Now, repent of your sins and come back to God." After Peter's sermon, more people repented of their evil ways and turned to follow after Jesus.

The early days of the church were not all joy and happiness. Some people still had too many of their old, evil ways about them. One example was Ananias and his wife, Sapphira. They had a piece of land and told the church that they were going to sell it and give the money to the apostles to help spread the Gospel. They did sell it but kept part of the money for themselves. For this, the apostles called them out as liars against God. It wasn't that they kept some for themselves that was wrong, but the fact that they were boastful about their charity to the church. Ananias was so grieved about being caught in a lie, that he walked out of the room and died.

As the church expanded around Jerusalem, the apostles began to get into more and more trouble with the Temple priests and elders, the same evil ones which had been directly responsible for crucifying Christ. The apostles were arrested, but an Angel came and unlocked the doors and let them out. The apostles came right back the next morning and taught in the Temple, right before the priests.

The priests met, and had the apostles brought to them again. They were very mad at them. The priests said, "You have filled up all of Jerusalem with this doctrine, and you are trying to bring Jesus's blood on us."

Peter spoke angrily for the group, and said, "We ought to believe God rather than man. YOU did crucify him, and YOU hung him on the cross! But God raised him up from the dead to be the ultimate payment for sin, and to bring the Holy Spirit, and we are witnesses to the fact that the things we say are all true."

One of the Pharisees there, a man named Gamaliel, very intelligent about the laws of the Jews, took the Priests aside and told them, "Leave these men alone. If it is all just an act or a lie, nothing will come of it. And if it really is from God, nothing you can do will stop it." The priests agreed and after they had the apostles beaten, they told them all to not speak in the name of Jesus anymore, let them go. Of course, the apostles went right back to preaching about Christ, going from house to house to meet with the believers meeting in their homes.

Most of the recorded expansion of the Christian church is attributed to the Apostle Peter. In one early episode, a disciple that was known as Philip the Evangelist went to Samaria to teach Christianity. A great many people were healed and believed, but nobody was being born again. It was a mystery to Philip what was happening. Then he encountered a man named Simon, a magician, who had bewitched the people there.

Philip was able to cast out his devils and convert him to Jesus as well, and many were baptized. Peter and John came up to Samaria to see what the problem was, and after they had laid hands on the people, they also finally received the Holy Spirit.

The apostle Peter was directed to go to a house of a Gentile in the city of Caesarea and teach him about Jesus. Caesarea was a port city on the Mediterranean, built by King Herod, and mostly filled with Roman citizens. Peter objected to it because he still thought that Jesus had only been sent to the Jews. Jesus came to him in a dream, showing a large net filled with all sorts of animals, including some which were considered unclean by the Jews. Jesus told him that what God cleaned, was clean, no matter what the Jews taught. So Peter agreed and went to the home of Cornelius, a Roman soldier. Peter taught him and his family about Jesus, and after he taught, the whole family got born again and began to speak in other tongues. Peter was amazed to see that the Gentiles too could receive the Holy Spirit as he had. This was the first time that Gentiles had been brought into the promised family of God.

The other apostles were at first mystified by the news when Peter told them about it. It went against everything they had ever believed. But Peter convinced them, saying, "What was I, that could withstand God?" After that, they glorified God, that he would give the Gentiles repentance unto eternal life also.

Now the church was expanding to the Gentiles as well, and King Herod began a persecution of the Church. He had James, the brother of John, killed. Then he had Peter arrested, and put in prison. An angel came and broke him out in a miraculous manner. He was being guarded by sixteen soldiers, and at night, they chained Peter to men on either side of him. The angel removed the chains in the middle of the night and Peter walked right out of the prison.

Peter and the other apostles continued to go from synagogue to synagogue, and from house to house, preaching the words that Jesus had taught them about. Many miracles were done before the Jews of the day. But there was even more to come.

33. The Conversion of Saul

So Ananias departed and entered the house, and after laying his hands on him said, "Brother Saul, the Lord Jesus, who appeared to you on the road by which you were coming, has sent me so that you may regain your sight and be filled with the Holy Spirit." And immediately there fell from his eyes something like scales, and he regained his sight, and he got up and was baptized.

(Acts 9:17-18)

O ne day, the priests captured the apostle named Stephen and brought him to the same courtroom to have him accused of blasphemy against the Temple— it was the same place that Jesus had been accused. Stephen gave them a long lecture about the ancient prophecies, how over and over again the people of the land promised to Abraham had rejected the words of the prophets. He talked about how Abraham and Isaac looked forward to the coming King and how Moses walked with God and how he had to deal with people all around him who were constantly rejecting God. Finally, in a fit of righteous rage, Stephen yelled at the priests:

You men who are stiff-necked and uncircumcised in heart and ears are always resisting the Holy Spirit; you are doing just as your fathers dd. Which one of the prophets did your fathers not persecute? They killed those who had previously announced the coming of the Righteous One, whose betrayers and murderers you have now become; you who received the law as ordained by angels, and yet did not keep it."

(Acts 7:51-53)

Stephen told them, "Now, you priests have rejected God and killed his son." Then. he looked up with sharp eyes and told the priests that he saw the heavens open and saw a vision of God, with Jesus sitting on the right hand of God. When he said that, it was the final straw! It took a toll on the said priests, as what he had just said jeopardizes everything they have believed in and everything they have done thus far—and they, being egotistical, self-righteous, unconscienced, mean, power-hungry men, they would not let Stephen get away with what he had dared to say and do.

After all that, the priests were enraged and had Stephen taken outside the city walls. They surrounded him, took off their coats, and put them in a pile before one of their young men. They threw stones at Stephen, who prayed, "Lord Jesus, receive my spirit." Then, he knelt down and said, "Lord, lay not this sin to their charge," and he died.

In the crowd, the young man watching over the priests' things was named Saul. He did not join in stoning Stephen, but he wondered about all the things that Stephen has said to them about the truth that the priests have so conspicuously denied and got enraged about.

Now, as the apostles and disciples spread the word far and near, word got back to the priests at the Temple and the Roman government that a group had continued to grow, and had become so big it could challenge their authority. Although Rome allowed many pagan religions to be practiced through their kingdom, when it came to these new people, who called, "Christ-Ins", because they were always preaching about Christ being in them.

It scared the Temple priests especially. Among them was a man named Saul, who had been raised in the synagogues of the Jews and was an expert in what the ancient texts, called the Torah, said. He was the same young man who was there when the apostle Stephen was stoned to death by the High Priests of the Temple and watched it all happen.

Saul was tasked by the Temple and the Roman government to track down where these Christian meetings were being held and to surround it with soldiers, and break into their houses to take everyone prisoners. Men, women and even children were arrested and jailed for practicing this outlawed religion.

Saul was committed to doing his job, thinking that he was right for trying to stop this new religion from growing. As the new Christians were terrified, they left their homes and spread out into other countries. This only helped to spread the news of Jesus Christ to other lands and other peoples. Soon people were becoming Christians throughout the entire eastern Mediterranean area.

Saul went to the Temple priests and asked them to write a letter of introduction for him, so he could go up to the country of Syria, where some of these Christian fellowships were being held.

Since he was working outside of his own country, the letter was asking the government in Syria to allow him to arrest these people and take them back to Jerusalem.

He proceeded with a group of soldiers and the letter in hand towards the capital of Syria, Damascus. As he got close to Damascus, a voice cried out from above, saying "Saul, Saul, why are you persecuting me?" Saul fell on the ground, asked who it was, and the voice told him it was Jesus.

Saul asked, "What am I supposed to do?"

Jesus told him to go into Damascus and wait there. When Saul tried to stand up, he found that he was blind. The soldiers helped lead him into the city and to find an inn to stay in.

Then Jesus came to a believer in Damascus named Ananias, in a dream. Jesus told him to go to the Street called Straight, and there find a man named Saul and baptize him. Ananias objected, saying that he had heard of this man, who had come to Damascus to capture and tie up the Christians there and carry them back to the High Priests in Jerusalem. He was afraid to do what Jesus asked.

Jesus answered him in the dream and told him not to worry, but Saul was a chosen vessel for him to bring Christianity to the Gentiles. Ananias agreed, and the next morning, when he woke up, he went to the Street called Straight and found the inn run by Judas and came to Saul.

Ananias witnessed to Saul, and told him all about Jesus Christ, what he had said and done, and what all the old prophets had said about the coming Messiah. Saul was very well educated about the Law and the Prophets—and eventually, Ananias was able to convince him that this was the man was the foretold Messiah. When Saul was finally able to believe, Ananias laid his hands on Saul, and immediately he was healed on his blindness. Ananias then baptized him, and Saul received the Holy Spirit.

Saul became really excited about Jesus Christ, and after returning to Jerusalem, he met with the apostles and the other church leaders, but people were afraid of him. They doubted that he was a Christian, but just trying to fool them so he could arrest them. Eventually, the apostles advised Saul to go far away, into a city called Tarsus in Turkey, and begin teaching the Jews there about Jesus Christ. Since nobody knew him there, he could witness to people and they would become Christians too.

Years went by, and eventually, people forgot about the bad things Saul had done. Saul changed his name to Paul, and the Apostle Paul became one of the most important teachers and writers of the early Christian church, writing many of the letters that became part of the New Testament.

Paul greatly preached around the eastern

Mediterranean, to spread the word of Christ to the Gentile nations. He traveled to Antioch in Syria, to Cyprus, to Galatia, then up to Galatia

When Paul was in Galatia, he was called by Peter to return to Jerusalem. The Christians there were still having an issue with the fact that Gentiles were entering the Church, that the Word of Christ was not only for the Jewish people. These objections were mostly coming from Temple priests who had been converted to Christianity but still held on to their old feelings. The leaders of the Christian church held a meeting, and Peter was able to tell them all directly what wonderful miracles he had seen about the Gentile converts. James, the brother of Jesus, determined that Peter instruct them against some practices that were in violation of the laws of Moses, to appease the Jews there, and to just be joyful that God had permitted the Gentiles to be added to the church.

Paul continued to teach, through Thessalonica

and Corinth in what is now Turkey, and later in Athens in Greece. During these travels, Paul commonly wrote letters to the churches throughout Asia Minor, which were voiced by the Holy Spirit. These letters became what is known as the Epistles in the New Testament. Paul had befriended a great ally, a young man named Timothy, who spend much of Paul's later years traveling with him and presumably helping Paul translate his writings from Hebrew into the common Greek of the Gentile lands.

Paul was often arrested, threatened, stoned, lost at sea, but he always relied on God. Eventually, Paul was imprisoned for years. He ended up in Rome and rented a house there for two years. It is likely that during that time, with his good friend Timothy, he translated the gospel accounts of Jesus written by the apostles from Hebrew into Greek, so the Gentiles could read them also.

Paul continued to travel around Asia Minor until

he got old, seeing a great expansion in the Church and correcting problems as they arose. As he got towards his death, the last letter that he wrote was to his good friend, Timothy. The letters to Timothy were full of great secrets about God and Christ because Paul trusted Timothy greatly to understand and teach what he wrote. His very last words voiced Paul's belief that Jesus Christ would return someday to wake him from death, and he would be made incorruptible:

I solemnly charge you in the presence of God and of Christ Jesus, who is to judge the living and the dead, and by His appearing and His kingdom: preach the word; be ready in season and out of season; reprove, rebuke, exhort, with great patience and instruction. For the time will come when they will not endure sound doctrine; but wanting to have their ears tickled, they will accumulate for themselves teachers in accordance to their own desires, and will turn away their ears from the truth and will turn aside to myths. But you, be sober in all things, endure hardship, do the work of an evangelist, fulfill your ministry. For I am already being poured out as a drink offering, and the time of my departure has come. I have fought the good fight, I have finished the course, I have kept the faith; in the future there is laid up for me the crown of righteousness, which the Lord, the righteous Judge, will award to me on that day; and not only to me, but also to all who have loved His appearing.

(II Timothy 4:1-8)

34. I Am Coming Soon

"Behold, I am coming quickly, and
My reward is with Me, to render to every
man according to what he has done. I am
the Alpha and the Omega, the first and the
last, the beginning and the end."
(Revelation 22:12-13)

When Christ ascended to heaven, he promised to return someday as Lord of Lords and King of Kings. Many, many people believed on his promises but eventually died—knowing that he would come again soon and raise them all from the dead.

The return of Jesus Christ hasn't happened yet, but it *will* someday. His return will happen in two parts. First, he will appear in the sky to bring home to him all those people who ever believed on him and were born of the Holy Spirit. Great trumpets will sound in the sky—and at the last trumpet, first, all those people who have died will be charged from dead, corruptible bodies into incorruptible ones. Then, all those who are still alive will be changed, in the blink of an eye, from mortal to immortal people. Then, everyone will rise together and meet Jesus in the sky. We will all go to heaven together and be with Jesus Christ forever.

When we get there, we will all stand before the bema seat of Christ. The bema seat is not a seat of judgment—but the word was used in the Greek language as the award platform during the Olympics. Christ will personally reward us for our lives offered to Him and give us jeweled crowns. We will know our old family members and friends and spend eternity together with our loved ones and make new friends, too.

Once all the Christians are taken off the world, a

terrible time will come for those who are left. The Devil will be able to do whatever he wants for a period of seven years, inflicting great pain on everyone. Terrible natural disasters will happen all over the world—but God has also appointed people to become new Christians during this time and bring as many people as they can to the knowledge and love of Jesus Christ. It is terrible that they must go through these horrible times, but God had promised that they, too, would live again with Christ.

Finally, at the end of the seven years, Christ and all the believers in heaven will go back to earth— and as one mighty army, they would defeat all the evil people and the evil spirits on earth. The devil will be chained up for a thousand years. Then, all the new believers from the last seven years will also be raised from the dead, and Jesus Christ and all the believers will live together on earth for the next thousand years as immortal souls, enjoying life together, rebuilding the earth back into a paradise like the Garden of Eden.

At the end of the thousand years, Satan will be released for a short time, but he will be conquered and thrown into an eternal lake of fire. God, who is all perfect Love, would even give the devil one more chance to repent and come back to God. However, the devil would instead make war against all of God's people, and God will cast him into a burning pit of fire—to be punished for all eternity.

Then, God would raise up every other person who had even been born and judge them according to their works. He would grant eternal life to people who had not heard of Christ but had done their best to be good to raise their families well. Those who had been hateful, mean people—God would make them vanish forever.

Then, God promised what the future of all eternity would be like:

*Then I saw a new heaven and a new earth;
for the first heaven and the first earth passed
away, and there is no longer any sea. And I
saw the holy city, new Jerusalem, coming down
out of heaven from God, made ready as a bride
adorned for her husband. And I heard a loud
voice from the throne, saying, "Behold, the
tabernacle of God is among men, and He will
dwell among them, and they shall be His people,
and God Himself will be among them, and He
will wipe away every tear from their eyes;
and there will no longer be any death; there will
no longer be any mourning, or crying, or
pain; the first things have passed away."*

*And He who sits on the throne said, "Behold, I
am making all things new." And He said,
"Write, for these words are faithful and
true." Then He said to me, "It is done. I am
the Alpha and the Omega, the beginning and the
end. I will give to the one who thirsts from the*

spring of the water of life without cost. He who overcomes will inherit these things, and I will be his God and he will be My son....

Then he showed me a river of the water of life, clear as crystal, coming from the throne of God and of the Lamb, in the middle of its street. On either side of the river was the tree of life, bearing twelve kinds of fruit, yielding its fruit every month; and the leaves of the tree were for the healing of the nations. There will no longer be any curse, and the throne of God and of the Lamb will be in it, and His bond-servants will serve Him; they will see His face, and His name will be on their foreheads. And there will no longer be any night; and they will not have need of the light of a lamp nor the light of the sun, because the Lord God will illumine them; and they will reign forever and ever **(Revelation 21:1-7 and 22:1-5)**.

Jesus Christ will rule this new *Jerusalem* forever—as King of Kings and Lord of Lords— and we will be forever by His side.

Conclusion

Thank you for making it through to the end of *The Bible Story Book For Kids*. Let's hope it was informative and able to provide you with all of the tools you need to achieve your goals—whatever they may be.

My little children, wherever you are, God is with you. Although you can't see God with your eyes or touch Him with your hands, you know that He is present with the joy and goodness in your life. You can talk to God without speaking a word. Just by thinking gratefully, you can talk to Him about the majesty of the stars, about the light and comfort of the sun and the moon, about the gracefulness of the birds and the beauty of the flowers, the freshness of cool water, the purpose and friendliness of your animal friends. You know that God hears you—by the fun you have at play, by the good food and loving care that He provides for you, and by the reward of happiness you receive when you are kind and considerate of others. May your daily prayers to God and gratitude for your blessings help you to always understand the power of knowing that God is with you—*always*!

Ultimately, may this book lead you to an understanding of God and of His son, Jesus Christ, to the point that you believe and confess Christ to be your personal savior—that you are filled with the Holy Spirit and given the promise of everlasting life.

"THE WORD IS NEAR YOU, IN YOUR MOUTH AND IN YOUR HEART"—that is, the word of faith that we are preaching is that if you confess with your mouth Jesus as Lord and believe in your heart that God raised Him from the dead, you will be saved—for with the heart a person believes, resulting in righteousness; and with the mouth he confesses, resulting in salvation.
(Romans 10:8-10)

If you have any questions about what you have read, ask your parents or guardian. They will be happy to talk about it with you!

Praise God and his son, Christ Jesus, Lord of Lords and King of Kings.

Amen!

www.ingramcontent.com/pod-product-compliance
Ingram Content Group UK Ltd.
Pitfield, Milton Keynes, MK11 3LW, UK
UKHW010627011225
9278UKWH00002B/2

9 783903 331166